EVERYTHING

L.M. Fuller

XULON PRESS ELITE

Xulon Press
2301 Lucien Way #415
Maitland, FL 32751
407.339.4217
www.xulonpress.com

Paperback ISBN-13: 978-1-5456-6516-9
Hard Cover ISBN-13: 978-1-5456-6517-6
Ebook ISBN-13: 978-1-5456-6518-3

TABLE OF CONTENTS

Introduction

WHAT'S LOVE GOT TO DO WITH IT?

In the 80s, a popular artist of that era asked a very profound question, "What's Love Got to Do with It?" She sang the song to a very catchy beat, and the single was considered—by some—to be her "comeback" because it catapulted her back into the spotlight after several years out of it. Her two prior solo albums might've failed on the charts, but this song, from her fifth solo album, reached the top five in both the United States and the United Kingdom. It even went as far as not only winning Grammys but also being inducted into the Grammy Hall of Fame.

With all this acclaim, it is quite safe to say the song's query obviously resonated with the public in a very profound and affecting way. What does Love have to do with it? Webster's Dictionary defines love as a strong affection for another arising out of kinship or personal ties, an attraction based on sexual desire, affection, and tenderness felt by lovers. Webster's also defines love as an assurance of affection, warm attachment, or devotion. The Bible itself mentions Love more than three hundred times. One such verse states that if we speak with human eloquence and angelic ecstasy but don't Love, we are nothing but a great deal of annoying noise. If we speak God's Word with power, revealing all His mysteries, making everything as plain as day, and if we have faith that can, with words alone, make a mountain move, but we don't Love, we are nothing. We could give everything we own to the poor and even lay our lives down for a great cause, but if we don't Love, we have done nothing at all. So, no matter what we say, what we believe or what we do, we will gain nothing, and have done nothing at all. We are totally bankrupt without Love (1 Corinthians 13:1-3 MSG)!

Love, or more accurately the *idea* of love, reigns within the hearts and minds of every individual on our planet in some way, shape, fashion, or form. Love is one of the single most powerful forces known to humankind. Whether it reveals itself through tenderness, passion, righteous indignation, selflessness, or blind irrationality, Love can overcome the evils and pettiness of life because it inspires, unites, and quite simply can change the world as we know it! The Power of Love is regrettably one of the most untapped resources on earth as well as the most misunderstood. This widespread misunderstanding has an agenda that is subversive in its nature. This miscommunication is deliberate, calculated, and designed to lead as many as will follow this line of reasoning to utter destruction. Thus, the reason for this book!

There is enormous responsibility involved with the choice to Love. Therefore, the agenda to divert society has been relatively easy in transitioning our collective cultural view into the dumbed down belief that Love is abstract or a kaleidoscope of conflicting emotions. The first part of learning how to Love is the awareness of Truth! Not personal truth, an acquired understanding, or a skewed reality based in emotion. It is centered on knowledge, assimilated from concrete evidence. Why? Because one can never fully understand what Love is or even begin to learn how to utilize it without Truth being the foundation. The pressing sensations of instantaneous gratification have ambushed our reliance on the Truth, as well as the fundamental need for accountability. Unfortunately, because the programmed, default position to believe the breakdown of unmitigated Truth is at play, Love is distorted to the point of rarely being understood or even recognized at all.

The goal here is to address the wrongs of what has been fostered upon the collective conscience of mainstream media as love and replace those misnomers with the Truth of what Love is, how to recognize it, utilize it, and therefore be empowered by it. In an effort to meet the mainstream mindset, many secular definitions and views will be taken from top online research sources like Dictionary.com, Webster's Dictionary and others. These information sources will be used here because they are more influential in swaying opinion due to their regular use and vast range of popularity. However, because many descriptions, meanings, and explanations in the content of these sites are not always based in Truth, but in opinion and agenda-based ideology, I will use scripture taken from the King James Version of the Bible unless otherwise indicated, as solid foundation throughout this book. Strong's Exhaustive Concordance of the Bible will also be used for translations and in-depth word study.

The objective and most fervent prayer throughout the following pages, is for the eyes of your understanding to become enlightened so that you realize, the correct response to Tina Turner's chart topping, Grammy winning, record breaking and Hall-of-Fame inducting question, "What's Love got to do with it?" —is EVERYTHING! The Message Bible, in 1 Corinthians 13:8, goes on to state that inspired speech will end someday and understanding will reach its limit, but Love will never die. Love quite simply is EVERYTHING. Thank you for joining me on this journey to find out why.

Chapter One

HOOKED ON A FEELING

"It must have been love, but it's over now!"–Roxette

B lue Swede, a 70s band, sold us on the concept of not being able to stop the feeling of being in love, because they were high on believing they were in love, because of being hooked on the feeling of being in love. Wow, say that again three times fast! Contrary to popular belief, Love is not a feeling. Whatever springs from emotion or chemical responses that may *lead* to or set one on the path of Love, the sensory perceptions or chemical responses do not, in and of themselves, in any way, remotely resemble what Love is. The willingness to jump on the runaway car of emotional upheaval that romantic feelings inspire is what fuels the stuff of fairy tales.

Billy Ocean, another singer from the 80s, used to think "love was just a fairy tale," and upon careful consideration, I am convinced that it was then and still is now. Don't get me wrong. Love (with a capital "L") *is* real. Only a choice few, who are willing to make the necessary sacrifices, will achieve what others can only aspire to read about in…well—fairy tales! Love is not that first excited response found in an initial glance, the first touch or spoken word. No, those properties describe attraction, chemistry, lust, and passion. While those are bold, intense, and compelling in their drives, they are not what define that true, naked, undefiled, and everlasting crazy little thing called Love. Love, quite simply, is a choice. This cannot be stressed enough! Maturity comes when we realize the commitment to Love must remain long after the *feelings* to commit to Love have long passed.

It is not at all about how you *feel* in a situation, but in what you *choose* to *do* in the situation that makes all the difference. If anyone tells you differently, I can guarantee they are trying to sell you something!

It is a premeditated campaign, this onslaught on our senses! It is a cultural accumulation of diabolical proportions. Our society emphasizes the initial reaction found in attraction, chemistry, lust, and passion. In turn, it purposefully and misleadingly defines them as love (with a lowercase "l"). This is calculated for the masses to miss the genuine and gravitate to the counterfeit. These highly charged emotions are not Love! From the highest hilltop, this must be screamed until it is embedded into our collective social conscience.

These sensory perceptions, wrapped and tangled up in immature energies, are subject to change at any given moment without provocation, rhyme, or reason. Such concentrated, awe-inspiring impulses are not meant to last. If they did, everyone would eventually drag around in staggering states of exhaustion all the time, debilitated by euphoria induced hangovers! To define something as fundamental, basic and lasting as Love on such a variable and shifting foundation shows very little wisdom and lacks the scope of true vision. This kind of love is indeed a fantasy and should not be labeled the stuff of fairy tales, but rather a horror movie on steroids due to the psychosomatic devastation and emotional fallout that follows.

People who believe they are "in love" tend to be highly susceptible. Our liberalistic society capitalizes on the predisposition to fall prey to the hype that line of thinking inspires. In short, it's called a Fear, Uncertainty, and Doubt Campaign (FUD). According to several modern online dictionaries, FUD is basically a tactic used in sales, marketing, public relations, politics, and propaganda. This FUD infusion is a strategic attempt to influence perception by disseminating negative, dubious, and false information in a calculated effort to achieve financial gain or shift personal loyalties. Just think about it! If you are encumbered by a mindset that targets your loyalties and encourages the disbursement of your capital, regardless of if it has you on the fast track to your own demise—look around—I can *guarantee* there is someone there to sell you something every step of the way.

People who believe illicit sex is love can buy condoms at any corner store as well as avail themselves of adult toy touting shops to fulfill any fantasy or curiosity. In turn, there are also Mayo clinics, doctor's offices, Emergency Rooms, and abortion clinics to treat the fallout of such behavior—not to mention the pharmacies ready to dole out the next new drug in order to treat whatever is being ravaged due to whatever unlawful or corrupt sensual pursuit is the current obsession.

For those individuals who believe love is showering one's self and others with gifts of all kinds, there are stores and national holidays dedicated for that as well. On the flipside of this avarice, there are institutions to deal with the negative financial consequences inevitable for the average person who falls prey to this deception. These consequences usually lead to navigating the deep and various caverns of economic ruin. A testament to this financial dissonance is the inception of numerous debt consolidated services and the rise in bankruptcy litigation to handle our nation's newest form of debtor's prison—credit card debt!

We could go on and on identifying all the different avenues in which people choose to chase the idea they call love. These avenues also account for billions of dollars in revenue for those who care only for their own economic return. While capitalism in and of itself is very beneficial and should be applauded, it is of utmost importance to realize that falling prey to free enterprise with moral turpitude is detrimental to individual growth and positive social advancement.

People who operate under a false understanding of Love, obviously won't know how to Love. These people are often very cold-hearted and predictably self-absorbed, which is why avarice is a universal result. It has been foretold that dangerous times of great stress and trouble will come; difficult days that will be hard to bear. When people, especially leaders, lust to obtain riches at any cost, they soon self-destruct. This brings trouble for everyone because the greedy desire for money and the willingness to gain it unethically is the root to all sorts of evil. By longing for money, some have wandered away from moral virtue and live to regret it bitterly there after (1Timothy 6:9-10 MSG).

They will become narcissistic, self-focused, lovers of money, impelled by greed, boastful, arrogant, revilers, disobedient to parents, ungrateful, unholy and profane! They will have no other course but to be unloving, devoid of natural human affection, calloused and inhumane, irreconcilable, malicious gossips, devoid of self-control, intemperate, immoral, brutal, haters of good, traitors, reckless, conceited, lovers of sensual pleasure rather than Lovers of God. They will hold to a form of outward godliness steeped in religious practices, but will deny Godly Power because their conduct nullifies their very claim of faith (2 Timothy 3:1-5 AMP).

Such people are to be avoided because they will worm their way into homes and captivate morally weak and spiritually-dwarfed people weighted down by the burden of their evil thinking and evil deeds. This will make them easily swayed by various impulses. They are always seeking knowledge or someone to teach them, but are never able to come into the knowledge of the Truth (2 Timothy 3:5-7 AMP). These self-absorbed, pleasure-oriented people seek anything that will feed their next fix whether it is edible, chemical or hormonal; and you know there are places turning a profit to provide every flavor in whatever rainbow one chooses to follow!

I know presenting statistics here would be an impressive way to further this argument. However, I've found statistics are relative to whatever is being discussed. We can always find data to support what we want to say. So, think about. Do we really need cited statistics here to prove the obvious? Just look around you! How many people do you know who have been flattened by the runaway train of cynicism after getting flung off whatever merry-go-round at the time was believed to be love? This could include yourself if you have any adult or even teenage years under your belt.

If you were not already aware, you are in a war! A war for your mind, your heart, your body and your very life! In this war, your adversary is rapacious, unrelenting, and determined to steal, kill, and destroy (John 10:10). The first thing to consider is your enemy in this avaricious war wants to convince you he is not real—he is a great deceiver! John 8:44 reveals this enemy as a murderer who does not stand in Truth because there is no Truth in him! He is also deemed a liar—actually stated as being the very father of lies. So, if the enemy can convince you he is not real, then it stands to reason there is no fight in which to engage. If there is no fight, it negates the need for a victory.

The second thing the enemy wants to do is to convince you that you are the most important thing in your life. It's all an ambush to confuse you about Love in an effort to set your feet on a path of mental, emotional, and spiritual annihilation. Walking in Love allows you to live in hope instead, leaving no room for fear (1 John 4:18). A well-formed life based in Love banishes a fearful life: fear of death, fear of judgment, fear of rejection. It opens the doors for understanding to flourish and for ignorance to wither and die.

We are made in the image of God, Who Is Love, so Love is the essential part of who we are (Genesis 1:26a; 1 John 4:8). There is enormous responsibility involved with the choice to Love. Therefore, our enemy's task has been relatively easy in transitioning our society into the simplified belief that Love is abstract or a chameleon of conflicting emotions. One such lie is that lust is Love. Another is that Love is blind.

Lust is careless, selfish, and only concerned with right now. Lust is what blinds! It causes you to see things the way you need to see them in order to blind you to actions otherwise unacceptable! Love, however, deals in responsibility and does not take for granted the inherent authenticity of events. You won't catch Love carelessly expressing itself on a whim with total disregard to any possible consequences. Love is far from being blind like that! If anything, it is Love that *clears* vision and sharpens focus, helping you see people and situations as they really are.

The framework of Love compels assessment beyond the moment to the morning after and all other days that follow. Love is born of choice and is then *expressed* through heartfelt emotion. The engagement of emotional sensations as sole means to undertake a course of action can lead to squander or disgrace. On the contrary, Love instead nourishes and protects. Love seeks the foundation of Truth instead of the false protection of deceptions (1 Corinthians 13:4-6).

This is probably why all those fairy tales *end* with "and they lived happily ever after," because *that* is where the fairy tale ends and the real *work* begins! Oops! W-o-r-k! Excuse this four-letter word. Another little-known fact in this arena called Love is that we cannot bypass the w-o-r-k involved. It is a necessary "evil" to ensure the permanent, fulfilling, and ever-increasing enigma called Love to flow. In all relationships, learning to accept one another's faults and choosing to celebrate each other's differences involves *choice* and is one of the most important keys to sustaining a real, healthy, growing, and lasting "happily ever after."

This is Love, and Love is choice, and choice is **work**! That sometimes vile word—work—is also accompanied with other uncomfortable ones like sacrifice, humility, commitment, and forgiveness, just to name a few. Notice that each word mentioned is *not* imbedded in emotion, but entrenched in *choice*. It is not at all about how you *feel* in a situation, but what you *choose* to *do* in that situation that makes all the difference! Hold on, that bears repeating one more time just in case you missed it the first couple times. *It is not at all about how you feel in a situation, but what you choose to do in that situation that makes all the difference!*

Less Is More

There's a difference between "Loving" and being "in love." Being "in love" can have its roots in *self-I-shness* because it is initially based on what you feel, or most likely what you perceive you are feeling at the time. Feelings change, sometimes so swiftly you forget why you felt that way in the first place! Don't take that the wrong way. Being "in love" is not wrong. This capricious feeling is just not what prudent individuals should base anything of value or importance on! It could be and most likely is a false positive because—as feelings tend to do—that "in love" *feeling* comes and goes.

This is why when all those "in love" feelings die down, people believe they have "fallen" out of love because they were in emotion or lust. The Truth is they have fallen out of feelings, especially in a romantic sense, once the physical needs fueled by that initial attraction or lust have been sated.

Loving, on the other hand, is established in *self-LESS-ness* and is fueled by a spirit of giving. Less is more in this case because it is based, not on feelings inundating you, but on the feelings you create in others through how you *choose* to treat them. Love is expressed in how you give of yourself to others, not in a physical sense, but a connective sense through words, thoughts, actions, and deeds.

The focus of Loving is not based on how others treat you, which brings us back to what can never be emphasized too much—choice. Now while it is true you cannot control who you are *attracted* to, you *can*, however, control who you *choose* to Love. Attraction fuels feelings (the concocted love: lowercase "l"), but *choice* fuels Love (the authentic Love: capital "L"). Being "in love" is based on feelings. Loving is rooted in selfless choice.

Albert Einstein once said, "When you trip over love, it is easy to get up. But when you fall in love, it is impossible to stand again." The whole phrase of "falling in love" should be a dead giveaway to its malevolence. Just think about it! As far back as you can remember, falling involved some sort of injury or at the very least a discomfort of some kind, if not being undeniably painful, right? So, why anyone would seek to fall into anything on purpose is beyond me! Seriously though, the choice to Love should comprise neither tripping nor falling. In retrospect, forward momentum to emotional attraction can lead to perpetual devastations when we leap before we look. Leaping before looking is emotion. Spontaneity is great, but it should not be the sole factor when determining the direction of your life or when the influences of that impulse can affect you negatively for several months, years, or decades to come.

For perspective, take the scenario of someone insulting you so vulgarly that you punch them in the face. Now while your sensibilities and emotions may have told you that they indeed earned that punch, it would be your body that gets arrested and dragged away in handcuffs on the charge of assault. It would also be you, who bodily goes before the judge to answer the criminal charge, with the very real possibility of being tried and convicted of the assault.

If so enforced, it would be your bank account from which fines may be imposed and, again, your body to which a little community service or even jail time might be thrown in for good measure. Not to mention a few anger management courses could be required—of which you may also have to foot the bill! The whole messy ordeal could have been avoided had you not allowed emotion to rule and instead made a more informed choice.

Anne Frank was very insightful when she wrote, "Our lives are fashioned by our choices. First we make our choices. Then our choices make us." The enemy of your soul wants you to believe you have no choice, that you are a slave to your baser nature. Remember, he wants to first convince you he's not real and by doing so, the fact that you are in a war loses its impact. For there to be a war, opposition must exist. So, if there is no opponent, there is no need to take a side or make a stand. Alexander Hamilton, Gordon A. Eadie, Peter Marshall, and anyone else who might've coined the following phrase were correct: "If you don't stand for something, you'll fall for anything!"

By not knowing or accepting the Truth, we are held hostage by what other people think and by our own unqualified instincts. If you can be convinced that you have no control over your own choices, you have already lost the war before you even realize the battle has been declared.

Living out the consequences of other people's wrong choices for your life by following their example should never be your aim. Let them deal with their own consequences! Instead, choose your way through an informed decision-making process fueled by God's Word and guided by His Spirit. Resist being led by the way of instinctual reactions. God instructs us to study and be eager to do our utmost in order to present ourselves to Him approved, a worker tested by trial who has no cause to be ashamed, accurately handling and skillfully teaching the Word of Truth (2 Timothy 2:15 AMP).

God encourages us to know Truth so that we won't be easily fooled into believing falsehoods or deceits. What you let in through your eye and ear gates will flow straight down the pathway into your heart. These influences will campaign and guide, but the ultimate choice is still yours based upon what you've allowed to penetrate your heart. In refusing to view or pay attention to any-thing despicable or vulgar, and having nothing to do with whatever goes against a productive path for your life, those things obsessive or not acquainted with Truth won't have as much opportunity to easily cling to you and influence you to make detrimental decisions (Psalm 101:3; Galatians 6:7).

We are constantly bombarded with the total distortion that Love has no choice, that we are helpless in the face of its merciless grip. Many elicit relationships are initiated through this feeble reasoning that the parties involved just "fell in love"—again, that implies helplessness or a false inability to choose! We must understand what constitutes Love. Feelings and reason could be deceiving. They can influence wrong thinking, which leads to flawed percep-tions and ultimately result in wrong choices.

Being governed by fleshly pursuits or driven by your carnal nature is not a state in which you will achieve victory or real hap-piness. That is going outside of Christ, and outside of Christ is where we have no choice. Yes! *Without* Christ, we *are* doomed to our baser nature! Only by repenting of our sins and accepting Christ's redemptive work on the cross are we made unquestionably free from sin. He conquered death, hell, and the grave so those who belong to Him can have the Power of His Life-giving Spirit that frees all who accept Him from the power of sin that leads to death (Romans 8:10; Romans 6:23 AMP).

In the eighth chapter of Romans, we are told that the law of Moses was unable to save us because of the weakness of our sinful nature. God did what the law could not do. He overcame sin and removed its penalty *and* its power over us. He sent His Own Son in the likeness of sinful man as an offering for sin. With this ulti-mate sacrifice, God declared an end to sin's control over us (past, present, and future sins)! He did this, so the just requirement of the law has been fully satisfied. Therefore, we are no longer obligated to follow the old sinful nature! Instead, we can follow a new, Spirit-empowered one. The Word of God is clear, without Christ we are spiritually dead and separated from God because of sin. None of us have the power on our own to overcome sin (Romans 8; Isaiah 59:1-2; Ephesians 2:4-6).

Yoga, transcendental meditation, and philanthropy will not elevate you to a higher conscious state or buy your way out of spiritual darkness. God has shown the immeasurable and unsurpassed richness of His Grace and kindness toward you by utterly destroying the potent grip sin had on you and has paved a path for you and all who choose Him, to become spiritually alive, together with Christ.

The Word of God is given by God's Divine Inspiration and is profitable for instruction, for conviction of sin, for correction of error and restoration to obedience, for training in righteousness and learning to live in conformity to God's Will, both in public and in private. It is not for condemnation or to point a finger at you to tell you how wrong you are. Immersion and adherence to God's Word, brings access to the Power found in God's Grace. Only Grace will make you complete and proficient, outfitted and thoroughly equipped for every good work. God's Grace, His lovingkindness and tender mercies are more than enough and are always available, regardless of the situation you find yourself in (2Timothy3:16; 17, Ephesians 2:4-6 AMP; Lamentations 3:23 NLT).

God's Power is perfected, complete, and It shows Itself most effectively in your weaknesses and inability to do what's right. Where you are missing the Mark of God in your life, take heart and be glad because you can yield to the Power of Christ and allow Him to completely enfold you and dwell in you. Yes, we are weak in human strength, and that is why God gave us Jesus. Through Him, we are made strong, able, and powerful when we draw from God's Strength and Ability, which includes His ability to Love (2 Corinthians 12:9-10).

Only through being spiritually alive in Christ will you have the wherewithal to be set apart for God's Great Plan for your life. This is God's Promise to you: "'For I know the plans and thoughts that I have for you,' says the LORD, 'plans for peace and well-being and not for disaster, to give you a future and a hope'" (Jeremiah 29:11 AMP).

God's Purpose is not hooked on a feeling, but He will spiritually equip you *through* believing, so the self-I-shness of the "What about me" Syndrome gets crushed under the boot heels of the "What can I do" Ministry rooted in self-LESS-ness. On this path,

He will Empower you to Love as He Loves and you will obtain the freedom to live a Life of victory, adventure, and fulfillment!

Chapter Two

THE PATH TO LIGHT

"I am the light of the world.
Whoever follows me will not walk in darkness,
but will have the light of life."
~ Jesus (John 8:12)

We've seen plenty of movies where the hero, when having to diffuse a bomb, must choose between cutting either that infamous red wire or the blue one. If cutting the blue wire diffuses the bomb, then cutting the red wire will have disastrous consequences! It is the same with Love. We've simply been cutting the wrong "wire." Proverbs 16:25 states, *"There is a way that seemeth right unto a man, but the end thereof are the ways of death."* In other words, we choose the wrong course of action, *calling* it Love, thinking it is the right way, but it is instead the way that leads to disastrous consequences. We must throw off the shackles of social conformity and get back to the basics.

The course of Love is neither for the faint of heart nor the swift of foot. Just as deep-water diving is unwise off the Gulf Coast without scuba diving gear, the shifting waters of Love should not be negotiated without having first placed *choice* over the matters of emotion. As stated in the previous chapter, that "in love" feeling is emotion. Again, there's nothing wrong with being in love! It's rather nice, in fact. The problem with being *in* love is when this *feeling* is not attached *to* Love. Emotions are meant to *enhance* the journey of life, not *set* your life's destination!

God alerts us to the precarious nature of emotions when His Word warns us to be slow to anger, to rule our spirit, to guard our heart and mind in Christ Jesus, and to set our mind and emotions on things having to do with heavenly things and not earthly (Proverbs 16:32; Philippians 4:7; Colossians 3:2). To run headlong into a situation following emotion and not Godly Wisdom based on biblical principles is like spitting in the wind! Sure, you got rid of the unwanted, but it is swiftly redeposited in an uncomfortable and degrading way.

In reading and studying the Word of God, the one thing that primarily stands out is the continued emphasis placed on choice. As a human being, your standard of living should always be based on Truth, as Truth will never change because it is right the first time! The Word of God is Truth. In 2 Timothy 3:16-17, the Apostle Paul, inspired by the Holy Spirit, states, "*All Scripture is inspired by God and is useful to teach us what is true and to make us realize what is wrong in our lives. It corrects us when we are wrong and teaches us to do what is right. God uses it to prepare and equip His people to do every good work*" (NLT).

God challenges you with the choice between life and death, between blessings and curses, calling on heaven and earth to witness the choice you make. God is even gracious enough to give the hint to choose life so that you and your descendants might live (Deuteronomy 30:19 NLT). This life God strongly hints we should choose is firmly detailed within His Word. Jesus Christ, Who is The Word of God, gives life to everything that was created, and His Life brought light to everyone (John 1:1-4 NLT). This is a powerful Standard in which to base all belief. God never created us to be automatons, but living, breathing, free, moral agents capable of deep, lasting, Loving relationships with Him and others.

Joshua, a leader of God's people, once confronted Israel with the demand that they choose between serving the gods of Egypt from whence their fathers came, the gods of the Amorites in whose land they dwelled, or Jehovah "The Existing One" who brought them out of the bondage of Egypt (Joshua 24:15-17). To serve God is to Love God. Jesus let us know that those who keep His Commandments—The Word of God—are those who Love Him (John 14:21). Choosing to serve God by keeping His Word is choosing to Love God. *LOVE IS A CHOICE!* It is a choice that must be made regardless of how one *feels*. Unlike attraction, chemistry, lust, and passion, which are emotionally driven, Love chooses with deliberate impact.

If you claim to be a Believer in Jesus Christ, one who has been called out by a Holy God, then you have been instructed to no longer conform to this world, with its superficial values and customs. You are instead charged to be transformed and progressively changed as you mature spiritually in the renewing of your mind. How? By focusing on Godly-values and ethical attitudes. In this way, you may prove what the Will of God is—that which is good and acceptable and perfect—in regard to His Plan and Purpose for your life's path (Romans 12:2; 1 Peter 1:16-19).

If you are a wavering or backsliding Christian, you must wake up to the realization that you are being puppeteered by a socio-liberal developed conscience, fueled by the enemy of your soul whose only goal is to steal your will, kill your ideals, and destroy your ability to thrive (John 10:10).

If you are into trends or the next "must-haves" this season and everyone to follow, you may want to take the time out to be still and investigate the corridors of your own heart. Check to see if you find any areas in which you are lost, feel condemned, or are in need. Please realize that this lack could be part of the reason why you've been cutting the wrong "wire." Perhaps you've been trying to fill the empty places yourself with excessive workloads, food binges, pornography, or shopping sprees. Having nice things is fine. The nice things having you is not (Mark 4:19 AMP)!

The Amplified version of Matthew 6:24 declares that no one can serve two masters. We will hate the one and love the other, or will stand by and be devoted to the one and despise and be against the other. We cannot serve God and deceitful riches, money, possessions, or whatever is the most current or fashionable god. The necessity to have and the need to acquire more are outward signs of an inward lack and that lack is brought about by a deficiency in one's ability to Love. For everyone has sinned, and we all fall short of God's Glorious Standard (Romans 3:23 NLT).

No one! Not you, me nor the most "bestest" of the best. NO ONE is exempt from adhering to God's Standard. He knew we were unable to do so in our own strength or effort of will, so God, by His Grace, freely makes us right in His sight. He did this through His only begotten Son. Jesus was sent into the world not to judge the world, but to save the world by dying so we would be freed from the penalty for our sins (Romans 3:24 NLT; John 3:16-17 AMP)!

If you find yourself in this quandary of being torn by two loyalties, I invite you to ask God to free you from the bondages of corrupted, immoral behavior driven by the lust and rottenness of this world. Whether you have repented of your sins and asked Jesus into your heart before or have never done so, I ask that you investigate the corridors of your own heart. Check to see if you find any area in which you are lost, feel condemned, or are in need. Please realize that this lack is a sign of the empty place in you that only God can fill. If this is you, please say the next words OUT LOUD and invite Christ's Love, forgiveness, and deliverance in today:

> "Father God, I come before You acknowledging that I have sinned against You. I ask that You forgive me of my sins. Jesus, I believe You died for my sins and that You were raised from the dead. I ask that You come into my heart and free me of the guilt of sin and make me acceptable to You. Thank You for saving me. Holy Spirit, I give You permission to lead me into all Truth and Empower me to live a Life hid with Christ in God. In Jesus' Name ~ Amen!"

If you believe what you just spoke aloud, YOU ARE SAVED or have rededicated your life to Christ! You are no longer condemned! You now belong to Christ Jesus or have been restored back to Him, and because you belong to Him, the Power of His Life-giving Spirit has freed you from the power of sin that leads to death. You've taken a momentous step forward. However, just as "Happily Ever After" doesn't just materialize with the turning of a page in real-life as it does with fairy tales, a life of Power and Freedom through Christ doesn't materialize that way either. We are admonished to work out our own soul's salvation by pursuing spiritual maturity, using serious caution and critical self-evaluation to avoid anything that might offend God or discredit the Name of Christ (Philippians 2:12 AMP).

This may seem an arduous and crucially burdensome task; and it would be *if* God expected you to do it in your own strength. Rest assured, it is God Himself Who will effectively work in you, to strengthen, energize, and create in you the longing and the ability to fulfill His good pleasure in the true purpose He has for your life—if you allow *Him* to Empower you to do so (Philippians 2:12-13; Acts 1:8 AMP).

A little-known secret to achieving "happily" will explicitly and without any doubt involve blood, sweat, and tears. That is a scary thought, right? Especially since you were just assured God will work it *through* you. Do not be afraid! Jesus has already supplied *His Blood* to cleanse you from dead works and unconscious adherences to your old way of doing things, as you yield to Him. The *sweat* is the effort that must be put forth by you to work out your own soul's salvation while, being strengthened, energized, and empowered by the Living God you rely on. As for the *tears*, they will be of joy as you obtain a Life hid with Christ in God (Hebrews 9:14; Colossians 3:3 AMP).

Still, it is easier to coast than it is to soar. It is easier to replace something than it is to restore a thing. It is easier to go buy something new than to fix what's already there. Buying something new means someone else did all the real work. Taking responsibility to fix what you have, takes **your** time, **your** effort, **your** commitment. Self-absorbed people don't want to take the time to do this because, quite simply, it costs them something. The key is to learn how to Love and to let It authorize the unlocking of every part of you, so you can inherit God's Best in every area of your life, mind, and heart.

The world is on a fast pace course to destruction because it follows the gospel according to man's doctrines, desires, and dictates. Our Gospel is hidden behind a veil. It is hidden only to those who are perishing. Among them, the god of this world (the devil) has blinded the minds of the unbelieving to prevent them from seeing the illuminating light of the Gospel of the Glory of Christ, who is the Image of God (2 Corinthians 4:3-4).

If you've spoken aloud and believe in your heart the invitation on the previous page, you are now a Saint in Christ, are no longer blinded and have the knowledge of Truth revealed to your heart (Philippians 4:21; 1 Timothy 2:4). However, before Salvation and the revelation of Truth, due to beliefs which originated in corrupt ideals, Love has all but dissipated as predicted in Matthew 24:12 (AMP): *"The love of the great body of people will grow cold because of the multiplied lawlessness and iniquity."*

If we as Christians, remain unaware or dispassionate toward this continual trespass upon the human conscience, the resulting emotional voids from which all forms of crazy ensue will continue to spiral out of control. Rome wasn't built in a day, but it was practically destroyed in one. Our home, our street, our city, our town, our nation, our country, and our world are no different!

Only through Christ are we able to obtain freedom from the power of sin and condemnation through Salvation, empowered by God's Grace. If you have accepted Christ, God now considers you to be one of His Own, part of His Family. You have taken on the Person of Christ, and He now resides within you. The fact that He was raised from the dead through the Glory and Power of the Father gives you the ability through Him to abandon your old ways (Romans 6:1-4).

Let go of the ways that have defeated you and brought you misery and shame and walk habitually in the newness of life founded upon hope and freedom. Your old human nature was nailed to the cross with Christ so that the body of sin would be done away with and you would no longer be obligated to behave as a slave to sin. The old nature has died, and you are free in Christ because His actions freed you from the power of sin (Romans 6:5-7).

The inability to Love is part of that old nature. The old nature, in cooperation with our adversary, has tormented and riled you to misdeeds or ineffective living up until now because you had not yet given your life to Christ or were saved but allowed your carnal nature dominance as one not yet yielded to Christ. If you have accepted Christ or rededicated your life to Him, this reign of terror is over! By God's Grace alone, His remarkable Compassion and Unmerited Favor in drawing you to Christ has saved and delivered you from judgment and given you Eternal Life. Be sure to understand that this Salvation is not of your own doing or through your own efforts. It is an undeserved, Gracious Gift from God and not a result of any good works nor attempts to do what you think is right, as you embark upon your Christian journey for the first time or as a rededicated Saint (John 8:36; Ephesians 2:8).

Now you have access to all you need to be successful in learning how to Love as God envisioned. Be warned, learning to Love will cost you something. The bright side is anything that costs, also has a return. When you pay the price, there is an exchange of some kind. Love is a Spiritual weapon, and because the weapons of a Believer are not carnal, the spoils of the war are not carnal either. They are Spiritual. Even though you walk in the flesh as a mortal, you cannot carry on spiritual warfare in the flesh by using the weapons of man (2 Corinthians 10:4 NLT).

Love's armament is divinely powerful, and It will tear down the strongholds of human reasoning and destroy false arguments. With Love, we can dismantle every proud obstacle that keeps people from knowing God, capture rebellious thoughts, and teach those thoughts to obey Christ. Love's price is carnal death and Love's exchange is Spiritual Renewal. Learning to Love brings an inner empowerment and clarity of thought, which supersedes human reasoning and produces Righteousness, Joy, and a Peace that surpasses all natural understanding (2 Corinthians 10:5 NLT; Romans 14:17 NKJV).

Myths And Other Bad Ideas

As we embark upon this journey, we are assured and fully equipped because the Holy Spirit is called alongside to lead us into all Truth! Whether you are already living as a saint of God, rededicating your life back to God, or just accepting Him for the first time, it is my prayer that a few myths and other bad ideas will be dispelled for you along the way. Webster's defines myth as a widely held but false belief or idea. The best way to free one's self from any false belief, idea, or otherwise is to become acquainted with the Truth. We are admonished to study and do our best to present ourselves to God approved, a worker tested by trial, having no reason to be ashamed, accurately handling and skillfully teaching the Word of Truth (John 16:13; John 8:32; 2 Timothy 2:15 AMP).

To reiterate, all Scripture is God-breathed, given by divine inspiration and is profitable for instruction, for conviction of sin, for correction of error and restoration to obedience, and for training in righteousness, as in learning to live in conformity to God's Will both noticeably and confidentially, behaving honorably with personal integrity and moral courage—all this so that the man or woman of God may be complete and proficient as well as outfitted and thoroughly equipped for every good work (2 Timothy 3:16-17 AMP).

Understanding what Love is will indeed equip us for every good work. The Word proclaims that between Faith, Hope, and Love, Love outdoes them all! The apostle John further testifies to the validity of God's Word as the guidepost of Truth by stating that we are sanctified through Truth and that God's Word is Truth (1 Corinthians 13:13; John 17:17 NKJV).

I also pray that you as a Believer are fully persuaded that God's Word is Truth. That It is living, active, and full of Power, making It operative, energizing, and effective in your everyday life. It is sharper than any two-edged sword, penetrating as far as the division of the soul and spirit, which goes to the completeness of a person, of both joints and marrow, which are the deepest parts of our nature. God's Word also exposes and judges the very thoughts and intentions of the heart (Hebrews 4:12 AMP). His Word is the appropriate measuring stick to meet out and plot a course to our selected destination in learning how to Love. The focal point is awareness!

Some people have died of carbon monoxide poisoning peaceful, and blissful unaware. Sure, it wasn't a torturous death—going to sleep never to awake on this side of life again—but however peaceful, *death* was still the result! In the spirit of John 8:32, it is my hope your willingness to know the Truth about Love far surpasses a cynical outlook on Love, thereby freeing you to the joy of Love's liberty and the fullness of Love's empowerment!

As mentioned before, the purpose of this book is to address the misnomers of what our enemy has fostered upon the collective conscience through mainstream media as love and replace this myth-information with the Truth. Consequences as well as the rewards are inherently linked to the choices you make. Please, take off the blinders of day-to-day complacency and strap on the mindset of introspection to actively negotiate the vestiges of your own choices. In this way, you'll position yourself to live on purpose as well as Love on purpose. The Joneses may be going to hell in a handbasket, so let's stop keeping up with them! Instead, let's follow the path that leads to Life. That path is paved with Love.

Chapter Three

A MANY CONFLICTED THING

"I wanna know what [Love] is,
I want you to show me"
– Foreigner

To earnestly embark upon this journey, we must slow down to make sure our destination is accurately locked into our Love-seeking GPS. If we do not have the correct coordinates, we will not arrive at the proper journey's end. We have established that Love is not a feeling and that God is Love (1 John 4:8). This makes Love the primary characteristic of Who God is.

We have the capacity to Love since, according to Genesis 1:27, we are made in the image of God, made to reflect His Nature. Any effort made to seek to Love outside of God's Character, Empowerment, and Nature will result in failure since He is Love and therefore Love's Source. The word "Love," here in the Greek language, is *agapē (*ä-gä›-pä), meaning unconditional affection or benevolence—charity. This is what God has for us and expresses toward us. The NKJV of John 3:16 eloquently states this fact: *"For God so loved the world, that He gave His only begotten Son, that whoever believes in Him should not perish, but have eternal life."* It is this sacrificial, unmerited choice made by God that defines the very depth and Power of Love. Love is basic and unadorned so when we try to *add* extra and unnecessary things to Love, confusion will inevitably ensue.

The simple definition of an adjective, according to Webster's Dictionary, is a word that describes another word—a noun or pronoun to be exact. As you know, descriptions are tantamount to the interpretation of the ones doing the describing and, depending on the individuals in question, wide ranges of conflicting interpretations will transpire on any given subject. An adverb can be even worse than an adjective because it describes not only an adjective (which, keep in mind, is already describing something), but also a verb as well as another adverb. To add to anything dilutes its properties making it no longer the original and subject to the understanding of the one doing the describing. It is the same with adding to Love. Just as God is God all by Himself, Love, too, stands alone!

When the prospect of various *"types"* of love is introduced as a legitimate concept to describe or define Love, it's no wonder we approach Love with little to no real understanding of its nature or purpose. You've probably heard of or have used the terms philia, storge, and eros, or, as they are more commonly referred to, brotherly love, familial love, and romantic love. Brotherly, familial, and romantic are all adjectives that *describe* the *type* of Love being *expressed*. Expressions of something are not its pure form. Even though traces or imprints of the original may linger, the new entity will not retain the full measure of the original's perfection.

For instance, water is classified as an inorganic compound and is colorless, transparent, odorless, and tasteless. When water gets colder than thirty-two degrees Fahrenheit or zero degrees Celsius, it freezes into ice and takes up about nine percent more space than its predecessor. Even though ice is formed from water, because the properties have changed due to the aforementioned factor, ice cannot and will not be able to have the same impact or affect water has even though its state was derived originally from water itself.

It's the same with steam. Steam is the vapor produced when water is heated to about two hundred twelve degrees Fahrenheit or one hundred degrees Celsius (at sea level). In this changed state, it becomes so light it rises. I'm sure you can relate through quick reflection over the years of having observed the opaque solidity of ice and the vaporous characteristics of steam. It is quite evident that these are drastic changes in each of their properties, and they no longer share visible similarities to one another even with both having originally once been water.

This is what essentially happens to Love when we distort its nature by introducing other factors, thereby changing its characteristics and in effect making the result something else entirely. Let's look closer at each of the aforementioned so-called love *types* in order to understand the erroneous assumption that they are proper interpretations of Love.

Phileo Love

Let brotherly love continue ~ Hebrews 13:1

Brotherly love, as briefly mentioned above is *philadelphia* (fē-lä-del-fē'-ä) in Greek. This word's root is derived from another Greek word *philadelphos* from which we get *phileo,* an adjective meaning loving brother or sister—or, in a broader sense, loving one's fellow man (both men and women) or community. By attaching this adjective to Love, it's now opened to interpretation by those who reference its meaning. Therefore, the vestige of Love's purpose has changed.

Before you get riled or indignant, let's investigate further. One look at 1 John 4:8 will tell you *"God is Love."* Love in that verse is agape. Hebrews 13:1 does not reference agape! Therefore, we are not referring to God's *Standard* of Love, but man's *expression* of love. Again, an expression of something is no longer pure. It is changed and therefore altered by degree. There is another more common designation for brotherly love, and that is friendship.

Proverbs 18:24 reads, *"A man that hath friends must shew himself friendly."* The word "friends" mentioned in Hebrew is *rea`*(rā'·ah), meaning brother, neighbor, or companion. Webster's defines friendship as the state of being friends, the relationship between friends or a friendly feeling or attitude. These feelings or attitudes are again subject to the interpretation of the one to whom they belong. This can be confusing in application to those to whom the expression is intended, but stay with me. I promise I'm going somewhere with this.

Storge Love

***Be kindly affectioned one to another with brotherly love;
in honour preferring one another***
~ Romans 12:10

"Be kindly affectioned" mentioned above, in Greek, is *philost-orgos* (fē-lo'-stor-gos) from which we get *storge*; this is known as the mutual love of parents and children as well as siblings, but it focuses primarily on the reciprocal tenderness of parents and children. Note, agape is not the word from which this definition is derived. Again, storge is a naturally occurring familial affection that is open to individual perception and personal consideration. This brings us to our last and most misunderstood, underinformed, and widely abused type—or expression—of love...

Erotic Love

I am my beloved's and his desire is toward me.
~ Song of Solomon 7:10

In Greek mythology, Eros is the Greek god of love. His Roman counterpart is Cupid. In searching out scripture, *eros* wasn't found in any word translations describing love, affection, or desire. Webster's defines eros as the sum of the life-preserving instincts that are manifested as impulses to gratify basic needs, as subli-mated impulses, and as impulses to protect and preserve the body and mind. Dictionary.com also describes eros to be a love con-ceived by Plato as a fundamental creative impulse having a sensual element, an "erotic love," or "desire." In Song of Solomon 7:10, *desire* is tĕshuwqah (tesh·ü·kä') in Hebrew, meaning a longing or craving. The popular view of Romantic love is the expressive and pleasurable feeling from an emotional attraction toward another person often associated with sexual attraction.

I believe a reason the Bible does not delve into this partic-ular expression of love is because it's a more colloquial concept than the other expressions. Approved male/female relations in the Biblical account appear to focus on interpersonal matches like family appropriated betrothals, which led to marriages based more on the needs of and advancement for the families in question, as well as advantageous acquisitions of wealth and power—not romance. One exception I found was in Solomon's Song where The Bible describes a premarital courtship between lovers.

Song 1:2 reads, *"Let him kiss me with the kisses of his mouth: for thy love is better than wine."* Love, here in Greek, is *dowd* (dōde), and its root means to boil. Heat is definitely the intention with the use of this word, and The Song of Solomon is unquestionably steamy in its revelation of desire. In the seventh verse of the second chapter, it is respectful in consenting to not rouse sexual intimacy until the time is right. We later find that right time is when they marry in chapter three.

So, What's the Point?

The point is found in Colossians 3:2-3, which basically admonishes to *"Set your mind and keep focused habitually on the things above the heavenly things, not on things that are on the earth which have only temporal value. For you died to this world, and your new, real life is hidden with Christ in God"* (AMP). The King James version reads to *"Set your affections on things above."* Affections, here in Greek, is *phroneō* (fro-ne'-ō), and it means to entertain or have a sentiment or opinion; it also means, by implication, to be mentally disposed more or less earnestly in a certain direction and to interest oneself, intensively, with concern or obedience. We are then instructed to turn this focus toward the things of God. That is *God's* Way, *God's* Will, and *God's* Purpose. This is an eternal focus!

We have been conditioned since birth to conduct our lives and judge our value by external circumstances. Christ came to reveal God's Kingdom, which is *eternal*, by empowering our ability to Love. It is imperative to understand that friendship, familial bonds, and romance are natural *expressions* and that they can form and be driven by forces other than Love. This is the point. When we choose to govern our lives by the external, in which circumstance and other people's actions set the course, the intrinsic values of peace and joy that lead to victory will elude and evade at every turn. The enemy of our souls wants us to judge our lives by the external, and since he is the prince and power of the air, he has great influence over circumstances and fleshly reasoning (Ephesians 2:2).

To automatically assume Love is in the mix when friendship, familial bonds, and romance are mentioned is an opening for deception. This unwise assumption can lead to utter confusion because the influx of man's reasoning culminates in various selfish manifestations. This fact feeds the aversion to arbitrarily attach "love" to them. They are impersonal, and they gain depth through the implementation of the ones expressing them. Again, depending on the individuals in question, wide ranges of conflicting interpretations will transpire in the enactment of these "love" expressions.

When we approach each instance in the framework of Love, the results will be entirely different and more productive. Learning what Love is and Its application becomes even more important when viewed through the understanding that Love is an equalizer. Love is unchanging and remains constant no matter who employs it! With that understanding, Love will then become the common denominator of empowerment so that we will be able to recognize when Love is being employed or when there is a failure in the implementation.

Let's use friendship for an example. If you have a friend who is constantly leading you into one misadventure after another, rarely keeps his or her word, and in more situations than not, leaves you holding the proverbial bag, is this friend operating out of Love? I pray you agree this behavior in no way illustrates Love! If this is a "friend" in a college scenario, perhaps you have the car or he or she has the connections or whatever—this "friendship" is not based on Love, but need or convenience.

Unfortunately, friendship has become synonymous with brotherly *love*! Herein lies the danger of attributing Love with relational situations because the relationship in question can have nothing at all to do with Love. I know this is a very simplistic example of that idea, but ask yourself, how many times have you been hurt or downright devastated over the mistreatment of your friend? It could be because of the misinterpretation our society places on the nature of friendship being an automatic carrier of Love.

As a Fine Jewelry Associate in a once popular retail chain, I witnessed a very heartbreaking event that illustrates the falsehood of wrong assertions placed upon relational conditions, especially having to do with family. Lost Prevention—the specialists who work to secure the retail store, monitor inventory, and apprehend shoplifters—caught this woman and her seven-year-old son pilfering what turned out to be around one hundred and fifty dollars' worth of merchandise. She was unaware that she was pegged and monitored about forty-five minutes prior to her apprehension.

During this forty-five-minute time period, she was observed and recorded loading her son's inner and outer pockets with all manner of items (mostly things she would wear or use). After paying for items worth about twenty dollars, she and her son headed toward the doors and were detained outside the facility. Several of us watched as she, only having paid for items on her person, acted as if she was shocked and had no idea these other items were in her son's possession. By placing her son in this position, was this mother acting out of Love or out of a selfish need for personal gain? This is a drastic example, but how often do we automatically attribute Love to familial bonds?

This brings us to the last example, the romantic cliché: "If you love me, you'll let me!" How many *love*-struck girls (guys too!) have fallen for *that* (can you see me rolling my eyes) line? This is the most overplayed of all misconceptions, and it needs a more in-depth answer on how Puppy Love can lead to a dog's life, so we'll leave it alone for now and pick it back up in Chapter Fourteen. The essential point here is that Love is not an add-on. It is not an addition to something else, nor is it open for interpretation or debate. Love is to be given without dissimulation (Romans 12:9).

The Greek word for dissimulation is *anypokritos* (ä-nü-po›-krē-tos), and it means, in its purest form, undisguised and unfeigned. Romans 12:9 in the Amplified tells us, "*Love is to be sincere and active—the real thing—without guile and hypocrisy. Hate what is evil, detest all ungodliness, do not tolerate wickedness; hold on tightly to what is good.*" Do you now see the point? I pray you do because Love stands alone. It is an equalizer that levels the field. Love's Standard is a non-interpreted, foundational Truth.

Love's Power is Spirit-driven. If we actively choose to approach every aspect of our lives from the standpoint of Love, our lives will change for the better. This means hating anything that would deter, mislead, or confuse and instead, holding tightly to the dictates and directions of God's Eternal Word—which should *always* be our standard and *not* man's reasoning. Many devastations allocated by the constant pitfalls and sucker punches of life will dramatically lessen, while others will be avoided completely. The more Abundant Life, hid with Christ in God, will be yours to seize, enjoy, and reveal to others. Stay out of sentiments that feelings foster and get into the facts that only God's Word supplies. It is the *only* Standard, and it is a Standard that stands alone!

Chapter Four

NINE-TENTHS

Have this same attitude in yourselves which was in Christ Jesus;
look to Him as your example in selfless humility
~ Philippians 2:5 (AMP)

"Possession is nine-tenths of the law" is a well-known epigram that means entitlements are easier to maintain if one has the control of something, or difficult to implement if one does not. This is an excellent way to describe perception. What you believe or perceive to be true will obviously supersede and govern your choices over what you do not know to apply or enforce. This, in effect, makes perception nine-tenths of your life! According to Dictionary.com, perception is the ability to see, hear, or become aware of something through the senses, a way of regarding, understanding, or interpreting something—a mental impression.

The high rate of divorce, child abuse, and senseless murders in our country's homes and on our nation's streets offer testament to the incorrect perceptions governing people's choices. Generally speaking, it is quite obvious a vast majority of people lack the capacity to Love, nor do they understand Love's importance. It is no longer commonly known that it takes character, integrity, and courage to keep commitment with something or someone you now find disagreeable where you first found joy or fulfillment. Character, integrity, and courage are resilient, but not spontaneous virtues. They must be cultivated daily. It takes these enigmatic as well as provocative, reinforcements to walk in Love!

God imparts these assets along the steadfast road to achievement, as you rely upon His Wisdom, through the application of His

Word. When you feel overwhelmed or find His requirements are unrealistic or too idealistic to obtain, remember that God promised to empower you! You are not alone. Trust in and rely on Him and not yourself. As a saved child of the Most High God, He promised never, under any circumstances, to desert you, give you up, or leave you without support. He will not leave you helpless, nor will He forsake you, let you down, or relax His hold on you. The act of seeking Him, coupled with the desire to be led by His Spirit, brings the empowerment of His Spirit to do all things (Hebrews 13:5, Philippians 4:13). His Grace will Empower you!

According to Dictionary.com, perception in the absence of natural judgment with a view to obtaining spiritual direction and understanding is called discernment. Spiritual perception is the ultimate discernment. The Bible calls it the Mind of Christ and assures us the natural, unbelieving person cannot accept the teachings and revelations of the Spirit of God, for the teachings and revelations are foolishness, absurd, and illogical to the carnal mind. The flesh-led mind is incapable of understanding Spiritual things because they can only be Spiritually discerned and appreciated. The natural mind is also unqualified to judge Spiritual matters. However, proper insight achieved with a Christ-like Mind found in the spiritually mature Christians' Spiritual Man is then able to judge, question, examine, and apply what the Holy Spirit reveals. An unbeliever cannot judge this revealed lifestyle, nor can an unbeliever understand the Believer's Spiritual Nature (1 Corinthians 2:14-15).

This Mind, the very seat of God's Own Discernment, will also heed the admonition to abandon love for the world's ways or its properties because it understands that loving the world squeezes out Love for the Father. Practically everything that goes on in the world—wanting your own way, wanting everything for yourself, wanting to appear important—has nothing to do with the Father and only isolates you from Him as well as limits access to His Power. The world is temporal, and therefore fading fast away; the same goes with everything that people crave. But whoever does what God Wants is set for eternity (Philippians 2:5; 1 John 2:15-17 MSG).

Discernment is the spiritual side of perception because it relies on Truth garnered from God's Word and is inspired by His Spirit. It comes not by what is perceived through one's own senses nor by what is led by emotion. It is this understanding that will cause you to accept your limitations by knowing God's Grace is enough. It's all you need. God is Love, and Love fuels Grace. Love's strength comes into its own in your weakness. The minute you quit focusing on your weaknesses and begin appreciating Love's Gift of Grace, Christ's Strength will be able to move and empower you through your weaknesses (2 Corinthians 12:9-10).

With the Mind of Christ, you'll take your limitations in stride and with good cheer. The restrictions meant to cut you down—abuse, accidents, infirmities, opposition, bad breaks—will no longer overwhelm you when you allow Christ to take over! In this way, the weaker you get, the stronger He becomes in you. Also, through His Word, God retrains your perceptions about yourself. Instead of being a nobody, you have been chosen for the high calling of His Divine Work. Chosen to be a blessed instrument to do His Will and tell others of the night-and-day difference He made for you; how He brought you from nothing to something, from rejected to accepted. This is another element in achieving victory over your adversary. You overcome and conquer him by of the blood of the Lamb and by the word of your testimony (1 Peter 2:9; Revelation 12:11).

There is a very apt and popular saying: "Let go and let God!" Don't lose your grip on Love and loyalty. You should figuratively tie them around your neck and metaphorically tattoo their initials upon your heart. By doing so, you will foster a reputation for living well in God's Eyes and the eyes of those whose lives you touch every day. Sincerely trust God in what He says and don't try to figure out everything on your own. Listen for God's Voice in everything you do and everywhere you go because He's the One Who will keep you on track. Don't assume that you know it all. Run from evil and instead, run to God (Proverbs 3:3-7)!

This strategy will not be easy to convert to after following the way you perceived to be the correct one, but it will be worth it. It takes practice once the choice has been made to walk in Love. If you've ever lifted weights or took part in strenuous activity, you've found that it got easier as you continued in the activity. It is a process of conviction that gains momentum as you endure the course, regardless of the roadblocks littering the path. To never give up is a *choice,* and remember, Love is based in choice, not in emotion (1 Corinthians 13:4-5 AMP).

The upside or downside of choice is that it is sequentially a catalyst for emotion. Emotions "show up" due to stimuli of one sort or another, which is the very reason emotions are so flighty and unreliable! They are fickle, nondescript integers in a vastly shifting landscape powered by human decisions, chemical or external stimuli. In other words, no matter what you perceive, decide to focus on, or are exposed to chemically or environmentally, emotions will show up to reinforce these energies.

Emotions are explosive and, upon ignition, will blast the shrapnel of whatever stimuli you have allowed entrance throughout your senses, bolstering or waylaying you with the intensity of a ten-ton bomb! This is why God admonishes you to fill your mind with His Word and to earnestly guard your heart (2 Timothy 2:15; Proverbs 4:23)! He encourages you to meditate on things that are true, noble, reputable, authentic, compelling, and gracious. He will inspire you to choose to believe the best about people (spouse, children, other loved ones, etc.) and where you work (your boss, co-workers, customers, responsibilities, etc.), instead of dwelling on the worst things about them.

As the Amplified of Philippians 4:8 states, *"whatever is true, whatever is honorable and worthy of respect, whatever is right and confirmed by God's word, whatever is pure and wholesome, whatever is lovely and brings peace, whatever is admirable and of good repute; if there is any excellence, if there is anything worthy of praise, think continually on these things, center your mind on them, and implant them in your heart."* We must concentrate on the beautiful things (even if it's only ONE thing!), give praise for them and then refuse to concentrate on ugly things to curse and complain about. We must put into practice the choice to Love. Once you make up your mind for the good or for the bad, emotions then follow (Philippians 4:6-7; Colossians 3:2; Proverbs 16:32 AMP)!

I am an eternal optimist, so with the exceptions of casual connections, booty calls, hook ups, or one-night stands, I do not believe the majority of people who become involved in relationships enter them with the intentions of harming the other person on purpose. With this in mind, it is astonishing how many people end up doing this very thing! Why? Why is this so common a practice in our so called enlightened society, especially among those in the Christian community? Again, no statistics will get quoted here—just look around! How many relationships have you witnessed (or experienced firsthand) where one person betrayed, misused, or abandoned the one he or she claimed to Love? It is because of the carnal mindset of self-preservation.

When we solely choose our own needs over the needs of others, we start down a path that will eventually put us up against the wrong side of an impulsive emotion called anger when our needs go unmet (Matthew 10:39; James 3:16 MSG). Anger is an emotion that can sustain or backfire on the one who chooses to use it in an attempt to propel them to righteous actions or disastrous consequences when they foolishly indulge it. This is why God encourages us in Ephesians 4:26 that when angry, we are to not sin by letting our exasperation, fury, or indignation last until the sun goes down. Anger is not wrong. It is a barometer for gauging one's moral condition. It can even direct you to Godly victory!

Samson's anger at being denied his Philistine wife led to a great victory for his people (Judges 15). Conversely, Saul allowed the anger spawned by jealousy of David to utterly devastate his entire household (1 Samuel 18:7-11; 1 Samuel 31:4–6). By indulging anger instead of choosing to Love, more harm will come about than the original occurrence (as with Saul, selfishness), which prompted the anger in the first place. Granted, people can do some really dumb and outright stupid things when they choose to act out in truly idiotic ways! However, we are encouraged to take the *action* to Love them in spite of themselves instead of *reacting* to them out of anger or frustration (1 Corinthians 13:4-8).

As already expressed, if you are a newly saved individual, it is my prayer you build a foundation based in Biblical Truth, which will support an ever-increasing structure of Spiritual maturity designed to fill you to the point of overflowing in your God-ordained path to walk in His Love. If you are a Believer who has become complacent in your walk with Christ or have just rededicated your life to Him, it is my prayer that the Fire of His Faith and the Amazing Grace of God through His Son Jesus Christ, the embodiment of God's Love, and the intimate friendship of the Holy Spirit, be with you now and forevermore (2 Corinthians 13:14).

Therefore, I urge you by the mercies of God to present your body by dedicating all of yourself—set apart—as a living sacrifice, holy and well-pleasing to God, which would be your rational, logical, and intelligent act of worship. No longer feeling the need to copy the behavior, superficial values, and customs of this world but instead, allow God to transform and progressively change you into a new person by renewing your mind and realigning your perceptions to the cognizance of Christ's. This new awareness will help you embody Godly-values and ethical attitudes as you mature spiritually. You will learn to know God's Will for you, which is good and pleasing and perfect (Romans 12:1-2 NLT).

This process is necessary to reach the level of excellence needed to fulfill the purposes and intent of God's Will for your life. The themes of popular culture that aggressively mold the acuities of our society run rampant in every area of our media from sitcoms to national news. We live in a society where *Scandal*s are sexy, *Bachelors* and *Bachelorettes* make "I Do" a punchline, we are excited to see *Walking Dead* people, we're instructed on *How To Get Away with Murder*, *Transparency* is applauded, and *Lucifer* is like a superhero fighting crime and saving lives!

God promises judgment will come to those who call evil good and good evil, who substitute darkness for light and light for darkness, and bitter for sweet and sweet for bitter. This insidious programming fosters bitter jealousy and selfish ambition in people's hearts as well as the arrogant disdain for moral codes. As a result, our collective conscience devolves into defiance of the Truth (Isaiah 5:20; Matthew 24:12).

Take time to notice and remember that we are ambushed constantly with visual and audio stimuli to be led by our emotions (FUD Champaign); so much so that no quiet is possible without actively seeking it. The reason is because in the quiet, as a Child of God, you'll realize the lies for what they are. God is about the real you that matters! Author and Pastor, Rick Warren capsulized this by stating, "God is more interested in your character than your comfort. He is more interested in making your life holy than He is in making your life happy."

Happiness is fleeting, as emotions tend to be. Holiness, however, is what transports you out of darkness and into God's marvelous light (1 Peter 2:9). Now *that's* something to be happy about! Psalm 91:1 assures that when you dwell in the shelter of the Most High God, you will remain secure and be able to rest in His Almighty Shadow, Whose Power no enemy can withstand. God will meet you in that secret place and He will empower *you* to Love! Choosing to Love is choosing God! Choosing God is choosing freedom! Free people aren't needy. As stated before, if anyone tells you differently, I can *guarantee* they're trying to sell you something!

Remember to recognize the signs. Needy people consume. They consume people (relationship after relationship, competitive drives, trampling whomever on the way up whatever "ladder" is being climbed) as well as products of all kinds (food, clothes, shoes, cars etc.). You name it, and I'm sure there is a proclivity toward it. People whose inner guidance systems are empowered by Love have had their base level reset to contentment, restfulness, and satisfaction—real Joy, not complacency. Joy is one of the Fruits of the Spirit mentioned in Galatians 5:22. Happiness is fleeting because it is an emotion based in situational stimuli, whereas Joy is sustainable because it is fortified by Truth and therefore empowered by God.

Joyful people want others pleased and fulfilled as well. Joy-filled people are about *people*, **not** product! It is a domino effect. Just as misery loves company, joyful people want others to join their bandwagon of peace as well. Contented people don't arbitrarily consume, wallow, or waste. They have learned to be satisfied and self-sufficient through Christ—to the point where they are not easily disturbed—regardless of their circumstance. They are equipped with Godly Wisdom on how to get along and live humbly in difficult times, and also how to enjoy abundance and live in prosperity. In any and every circumstance, they have learned the secret of facing life, whether well-fed or going hungry, whether having an abundance or being in need (Philippians 4:11-12 AMP).

Unfortunately, the mindset of contentment (which can only manifest when people walk in Love) in a socio-liberal society where self is god, and things are entitled, is totally unacceptable, frowned upon and discouraged. Therefore, the main focus, the chief theme, and the directed course is dissatisfaction, which in turn fuels avarice! This cannot be stressed enough! One focus has external value and short-term advantages with economic benefit for the few, while the other, more peaceable and spiritually enlightened road, leads to benefits that cannot be directly measured in economic advantage but in mental, physical, and spiritual prosperity that lasts a lifetime, for the many. God Promises your body will glow with health and that your very bones will vibrate with Life when you choose His Way—the Way of Love (Proverbs 3:5-8)!

When you honor God with everything you own and all that you are, and when you give Him the first and the best, He will make sure your barns will burst and your wine vats will brim over (Proverbs 3:9-10 AMP). Barns are the equivalent of wealth stores or bank accounts, and the mentioned wine is the correspondent of Spiritual enlightenment.

The bottom line is that perception is nine-tenths of your Life! Whatever you believe in your heart will govern the direction of your life's path. Choosing Love, choosing God's Way, will bring you mental and emotional stability as well as tremendous Spiritually-ordained direction. This will lead to success and wellbeing—spiritually as well as physically. Choosing Love is choosing Life!

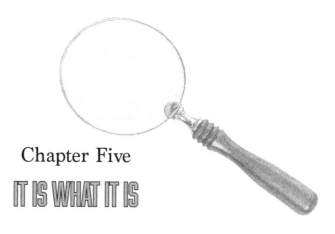

Chapter Five

IT IS WHAT IT IS

**Love bears all things, believes all things, hopes all things,
and endures all things. Love never fails!
~ 1 Corinthians 13:7-8a**

Anyone who has been in or around church knows about 1 Corinthians' definition of Love. The King James Version of the Bible calls it Charity and rightly so:

> *Charity suffereth long,* and is kind; charity envieth not; charity vaunteth not itself, is not puffed up, *⁵ doth not behave itself unseemly, seeketh not her own, is not easily provoked, thinketh no evil; ⁶ rejoiceth not in iniquity, but rejoiceth in the truth; ⁷ beareth all things, believeth all things, hopeth all things, endureth all things.⁸ Charity never faileth.*
>
> ~ 1 Corinthians 13:4-8a

I'm very partial to the Amplified version which reads: "*Love endures with patience and serenity, [Love] is kind and thoughtful, and is not jealous or envious; [Love] does not brag and is not proud or arrogant. [It] is not rude; [It] is not self-seeking, [It] is not provoked, nor overly sensitive or easily angered]; [It] does not take into account a wrong endured. [It] does not rejoice at injustice, but rejoices with the truth, when right and truth prevail]. [Love] bears all things,[regardless of what comes, believes all things looking for the best in each one, hopes all things, remaining steadfast during difficult times, endures all things without weakening. [Love] never fails [It] never fades nor ends.*"

Wow! That is so powerful! It is also very *impossible* to perpetually emulate without God! Man's reasoning toward Love eventually says, "I'm *not* going to take this, I *don't* have to take this, or I'm too old for this $%#@!" God's View on Love, the only view that counts by the way, is impossible to sustain without His Empowerment. Man's way says pull back, but God's Way says press through. Each view directly opposes the other.

As stated in the last chapter, perception is indeed nine-tenths of a life. The view or process with which you choose to address life, and the method in which you approach any given situation, is central to its failure or the key to its success. Unfortunately, a person's perceptive and emotional faculties, born in sin and shaped in iniquity, are primed to rule and govern from the beginning of life (Psalm 51:5). If there has been no Word of God or understanding of that Word in your life, the secular self of reasoning and instinct is all you've known.

Up until Salvation, there was no governing Spirit of God within you, nor any way to translate to your spirit any Gospel you may or may not have been exposed to. Nothing was in place to help challenge or disabuse your flesh of any God-opposing impulses or proclivities (1 Corinthians 2:13-14). Therefore, too many relationships break down on every level and fail to endure the test of time. Take heart though, as a Believer, you are dead to this old way and are now alive—through Christ—to a better way of thinking and functioning (Romans 6).

The mistake we make is to continue living as though we are not changed. To continue to live your life today, the same way you did before you repented of your sins and asked Jesus into your heart, is like putting on dirty, smelly, maggot-infested clothing after a long luxurious bath or day at the spa. It would be unthinkable, right? Jesus gave an illustration in Luke 5:36-38: *"No one tears a piece of cloth from a new garment and uses it to patch an old garment. For then the new garment would be ruined, and the new patch wouldn't even match the old garment. And no one puts new wine into old wineskins. For the new wine would burst the wineskins, spilling the wine and ruining the skins. New wine must be stored in new wineskins"* (NLT).

The old garment and old wineskin in this parable are the old life shackled to the law of sin and death; the one Christ sacrificed His Life to free you from with the Gift of God's Grace. The new garment and new wine are your new life in Christ. Living your life under the law of sin and death, now that you have been freed through the Law of the Spirit of Life in Christ, is like putting new wine in old wineskins or trying to patch an old garment with new fabric that does not match. The mindset and perceptions with which you've governed your life up to the point of Salvation must be reevaluated through the Light and Life found in God's Word. Nothing less will do.

You are called to a higher Standard as a child of God. Luke 5:39 states, *"And no one, having drunk old wine, immediately desires new; for he says, 'The old is better"* (NKJV). This is human nature. The old way seems easier because it has become habit; it is all you've known. To paraphrase Albert Einstein, "if you stick to your old way of doing things, you'll continue to get the same old results." Just because it's the only way you know, and therefore convenient, should not be the reason you stay on that path. Enlightened understanding will promote the desire for change because lack of Godly Change disproves the prerequisites of Grace.

Your old self has been crucified with Christ. It is no longer you who live, but Christ now lives in you. The life you now live in your earthly body is to be lived by adhering to, relying on, and completely trusting in the Son of God (Who is the Word of God). Do not treat the Grace of God as meaningless by continuing in your own way. If by remaining under the law or doing things your own way could make you right with God, then there wouldn't have been a need for Christ to die (Galatians 2:20-21). Don't give way to legalism. Only Grace will get you to the desired end.

To further illustrate this point, think of a computer. A computer is only as good as its operating system. If you know anything about customizing any system, you know the default settings (the original system's settings) are changed on purpose by the user when other options are chosen. Your default settings are carnal, worldly, and steeped in ungodly self-centeredness, and that's *BEFORE* you ever learn new bad habits from family and friends! Through God's saving Grace, you have been upgraded and now need new software adjustments just as a computer system would. This is a purposeful and directed transition that must be freely made so Love can reign supreme in your life.

The Bottom Line

The word "charity" as mentioned before, in the Greek is *agapē* (ä-gä›-pā), meaning unconditional affection or benevolence: Love. Starting at 1 Corinthians 13:4, using Strong's Concordance, let's break down each word in its original Greek to expand its meaning for a greater understanding of God's definition of Love.

It is **Longsuffering**: *makrothymeō* (mä-kro-thü-me'-ō) It does not lose heart, is long-spirited, factually forbearing and intuitively patient.

Kind: *chrēsteuomai* (khrä-styü'-o-mī) It shows itself useful and acts benevolently or graciously. Webster's defines *useful* as serviceable for a valuable or productive end or purpose and goes on to define it as being benevolent and gracious, organized for the purpose of doing good.

Not **Envious**: *zēloō* (zā-lo'-ō) It does not heat or boil with hatred or anger, nor does it earnestly desire, strive after, or busy itself about others.

Vaunteth not: *perpereuomai* (per-pe-ryü'-o-mī) It does not boast about or display itself, nor employs verbal embellishments to excessively praise itself.

Is not **puffed up**: *physioō* (fü-sē-o'-ō) It does not bear itself loftily, proud; it does not have an overinflated, swollen ego or opinion of itself.

Does not **behave unseemly**: *aschēmoneō* (ä-skhä-mo-ne'-ō) It does not act in an unbecoming or disgraceful way.

Seeketh not her **own**: *zēteō* (zā-te'-ō) / *heautou* (he-au-tü') It does not think, meditate, reason, or enquire into or to worship itself.

Is not easily **provoked**: *paroxynō* (pä-ro-ksü'-nō) It's not easily irritated, exasperated, or aroused to anger.

Thinketh no **evil**: *logizomai* (lo-gē'-zo-mī) / *kakos* (kä-ko's): It does not consider, take into account, weigh, or meditate on the troublesome, injurious, pernicious, destructive, wrong, or wicked.

Rejoiceth not in **iniquity**: *chairō* (khī'-rō) / *adikia* (ä-dē-kē›-ä) It's not exceedingly glad about nor hail injustice, unrighteousness of heart and life, or deeds violating law and justice.

But instead **rejoiceth** in the **truth**: *sygchairō* (sun-khī'-rō) / *alētheia* (ä-lā›-thā-ä) It congratulates and takes part in the joy of an honest mind, which is free from affection, pretense, simulation, falsehood, and deceit.

It **beareth** **all things**: *stegō* (ste'-gō) / *pas* (pä's) It keeps secrets or confidences and protects by covering over to keep off something that threatens and preserves everything, individually and collectively, the whole.

It **believeth** **all things**: *pisteuō* (pē-styü'-ō) / *pas* (pä's) It is propelled by moral conviction and persuaded to place confidence and trust in God regarding everything.

It **hopeth** **all things**: *elpizō* (el-pē'-zō) / *pas* (pä's) It waits for salvation or deliverance with joy and full confidence in God, regarding everything.

It **endureth** **all things**: *hypomenō* (hü-po-me'-nō) / *pas* (pä's) It remains, perseveres, abides, and does not recede or flee under misfortunes and trials, but holds fast to faith in Christ in everything.

41

Charity never **faileth**: *agapē* (ä-gä'-pā) / *ekpiptō* (ek-pē'p-tō) It is unconditional affection or benevolence that does not fall powerless; it does not fall to the ground or be without effect.

Back to Basics

It is my prayer that you have accepted and understand *what* Love is and what it is *not*. With this established, we can go on to explore avenues which adequately impart this most vital aspect to living a complete life; one designed to galvanize you as you reach your maximum potential. You may question: "How will Love do this? What is the key? How are you supposed to tap into the very deep reservoir of Love's restoration?" Whether you've just recently given yourself to Christ or have been saved for decades, the answer to this question again is, by getting back to the basics! Choice is key!

We are made as vessels of choice, which is why we are spiritual, intellectual, reasoning, and sentient individuals equipped with free will. This is the reason there was a certain tree placed in the Garden of Eden. The Tree of the Knowledge of Good and Evil had no inherent powers or mystical properties (Genesis 2:17). Its placement was a strategic way to exercise free will. It was a way to introduce choice: to obey or to disobey. Adam and Eve's decision to disobey, not the fruit itself, is what brought upon them the knowledge of good and evil. We were not designed with a hive-like mind nor were we intended to toe a line through rote behavior. We must fight the programming that is destroying the very fabric of our society and our ability to thrive. Look around you! Life is happening! Whether you choose to take part in it or not won't halt its progression.

In other words, life happens daily with or without your input. Since you must eventually deal with the consequences as well as bask in the rewards, why not wake up and take an active part in your Life's course? Following feelings are tantamount to building sandcastles in the sky; it's like having an elaborate strategy without a solid network in which to implement the design. We are

IT IS WHAT IT IS

admonished in Philippians 3:14 to press on to reach the end of the race and receive the heavenly prize for which God, through Christ Jesus, is calling us. Emotions and carnally-driven reasonings won't get us there as unscathed and refined as the God-empowered choice to walk in Love will!

What does this mean exactly? Does it mean to put up with people's crap? To allow them to walk on you, step on you, and kick you around? The Word of God states we are to not get involved in foolish, ignorant arguments that only start fights. As a servant of the Lord, you must not quarrel, but must be kind to everyone, being able to teach, and be patient with difficult people; gently instructing those who oppose the truth by our Christ like example. By doing so, perhaps God will change those people's hearts, and they will learn the truth. Then they may even come to their senses and escape from the devil's trap. For they have been held captive by him to do whatever evil he wants (2 Timothy 2:23-26 NLT).

Above all, seek God concerning your issues, but primarily, take personal account as to what the choice to Love says is your role in the resolution. This is the key! I know that finding the swiftest route to victimhood is trés chic in our culture these days; nevertheless, it is not conducive to living a victorious life. Seeking or accepting victimhood does not contribute positively to the lives of those choosing this route, nor does it aide in helping them become vital influences in our society. Taking personal responsibility will always remove you from victim status to victor standing because Love is Powerful! It Never Fails!

Chapter Six

A FAILURE TO LOVE

"Where there is love, there is pain!"
~ Spanish Proverb

The myth that choosing to Love causes pain has deceived people into making wrong choices and has erroneously led them down self-destructive paths. This duplicity resigns them to the ranks of victims in need of rescuing instead of the level of victors with the ability to combat the odds in order to obtain the goal of a fulfilled life. Love *EMPOWERS, STRENGTHENS,* and *ENLIGHTENS,* so the actual perpetrator in triggering the pain surrounding Love is not the choice *to* Love, but in choosing *NOT* to Love. It is a *failure* to Love that mimics a cancerous cell.

This failure is like a malignant tumor that destroys people's lives. It robs them of sound judgment, limits their authority, and weakens their spirit every time the choice to Love is denied. A failure to Love follows many different paths, and there are three very prevalent ones eating away at the very fabric of our human condition. This chapter will deal with the first path I believe is the catalyst, propelling most along the destructive course to withhold Love.

A Failure to Accept Others' Free Will

Hopefully at this point, it has been solidified within your heart that Love is a choice and not an emotion. With choice being the foundation of Love, a freshness will accompany every resolution to Love because it galvanizes hope and instigates joy in the hearts of those who take advantage of the wisdom to employ it. When you choose to Love, you choose God's Empowerment to accept (not condone or enable) other's shortcomings because the humility of Christ within you will reveal your own deficiencies in vivid detail to help you to realize, just as the one to whom you are passing judgment, you too fall short of God's Standard (Romans 3:23).

This realization assists you in not falling prey to the illusion of having the power to effectively, or on a long-term basis, control another person's thoughts and actions. By being fully aware you are who you are by God's Grace alone, instead of seeking to conform others to your finite ideas of who they should be, you'll seek His Standard for who *you* are to be through Christ Jesus (1 Corinthians 15:10).

Enabling and acceptance are in no way synonymous. Acceptance is realizing the limitations of your impact upon another's free will. It is deciding to do what is necessary on your part for a positive and productive outcome through the impartation of Truth, understanding, and compassion, regardless of the person's willingness to comply with your expectations by bending to your will. Enabling, however, is selecting to ignore Truth and actively assist wrong choices by making excuses for unacceptable or destructive behaviors.

Acceptance, on the other hand, edifies individuals. It takes notice of where they are in opposition to Truth and creates an atmosphere for positive elevation from error to Truth. Acceptance creates a platform that opens the door for invested growth. Meanwhile, in an attempt to avoid hurt feelings, condoning restricts the avenues for imparted Truth and, in turn, enables a web of deceit, which will eventually cause the inevitable hurt feelings as well as abolish trust when the Truth is revealed.

I enjoyed watching *The Jeffersons*, an American sitcom that aired on CBS between 1975 and 1985. One particular episode comes to mind that I believe perfectly illustrates this premise. The wife, affectionately called Weezy, played by the late Isobel Sanford, discovered painting. It turns out she had no talent whatsoever! I mean it was awful! I'm an Artist who uses several mediums and have won awards for my work, so I'm confident in saying her work looked like a toddler painting in the dark using a non-dominant hand during an earthquake! Yeah! It was really bad!

Instead of accepting she had no talent and letting her down gently with the truth that she should work a bit harder or find another hobby, her husband George (the late Sherman Hemsley) and her other friends lauded her talent as if she had great skill. They gushed and oowed and awed over this atrocious painting, but their wisecracking, loudmouth, and somewhat acerbic yet always hysterical maid Florence (Marla Gibbs), told her the truth.

With everyone telling her she had talent besides Florence, who tended to be difficult anyway, Weezy decided to have an art showing for the rest of the tenants in the building (the same building they had moved on up to get their deluxe apartment in the sky). Weezy wanted the other tenants to share and bask in her celebrated skill. People did come, but they were appalled at how bad the painting was, yet too polite to say so. As Weezy beamed over what she believed to be awe at her skill, instead of the stunned disbelief in how dreadful it really was, a man who was visiting one of the other tenants at the time walked in and was utterly amazed as he gazed upon what we believed to be a horrendous painting.

He marveled at how exquisite and perfect and awe-inspiring it was and wanted to buy it on the spot! Delighted, Weezy agreed to sell. Now, not only was she talented, but that talent was going to pay off with a sale! She sold the painting, and the man promptly pulled out a Swiss Army Knife and cut the canvas out of the frame, tossed it aside, and began walking away. Stunned, Weezy called out, "Don't you want the painting?" The man declined, revealing how bad he thought the painting was and that the frame had been the prize he'd wanted to snatch up all along!

Not only devastated, Weezy was also utterly humiliated upon finally realizing the truth. The painting was awful—so awful that the man had to cut it out and dispose of it on the spot before leaving with the frame. All had enabled her! All except Florence, who had accepted she had no talent and told her the truth! Enabling non-existent art talent and enabling flawed personality traits or moral codes are not in the same league, but I hope you get the analogy.

Enabling others as well as failing to accept others' freewill can create a long and painful walk on a short, rickety pier over shark infested waters! This course can lead to high blood pressure, anxiety attacks, severe migraines, and all manner of stress-induced and anxiety-ridden issues that impair and might eventually kill those who choose this path. This is mostly an emotional, mental, and spiritual death that does, on occasion, lead to actual physical death associated with the ailments already mentioned—including cancer, according to medical journals! Again, I won't bore you with statistics and ask that you just look around you. The increase in sicknesses, mental illnesses, and erratic behaviors you witness in others, or even in yourself, is self-explanatory.

Feelings from within or being out of control, as well as outer forces seeking to control, inevitably cause the flesh to want to escape. If not an actual physical withdrawal, then a mental, emotional, or chemical one will ensue. Adultery, gambling, alcoholism, and drug abuse are all derivatives of coping mechanisms widely used as an imprudent attempt to escape a real or perceived locking down of personal choices. This is why it is paramount to not allow ungodly thoughts and feelings to decide your fate, but to instead allow Faith to guide your actions.

When you try to exercise your will over the will of another who, just like you, has the right to choose, you are taking on a responsibility that is not yours, nor one you can sustain long-term. We are not answerable for grown persons who are capable of being responsible for themselves. Even a parent's job is not to control their child, but to teach the child to control him/herself (more on this in Chapter Thirteen)!

Refusing to accept what Thomas Jefferson so eloquently stated in the Declaration of Independence, "We hold these truths to be self-evident, that all men are created equal, that they are endowed by their Creator with certain unalienable Rights, that among these are Life, Liberty and the pursuit of Happiness," we doom ourselves and others to a diminutive life full of imperfect love. Jesus gave His Life to protect our right to choose, and we do not have the authority to then usurp Christ by imposing our needs, our wants, or our will onto another individual as finite as we are ourselves.

This is a form of rebellion. As 1 Samuel 15:23 reads, *"For rebellion is as the sin of witchcraft, and stubbornness is as iniquity and idolatry. Because thou hast rejected the Word of the Lord, He hath also rejected thee..."*

The compulsion to commandeer another person's will is deeply-rooted in fear and is, therefore, in total opposition to Love. This is a serious offense. There is no fear or dread in Love. Full-grown, complete, perfect Love puts fear outside of self and expels every trace of fright or trepidation. We fear because we inwardly believe we will be castigated or reviled, and in so doing we expose the fact of having not reached the full maturity of Love's complete perfection (1 John 4:18 AMP).

This kind of fear comes when we allow the pride of believing we'll be able to protect ourselves from hurt if we control the situation. This faulty thinking is caustic to one's emotional stability because pride goes before destruction, and haughtiness before a fall (Proverbs 16:18 NLT). Relationships are undermined when we seek to control them. Not accepting a person as is can break down the very building blocks that establish truthful interaction. When we allow grown people the God-given right to choose for themselves by allowing them to make their own mistakes and accepting they have the power as well as the right to do so, we open an avenue to establish proper allocation of emotional investment and mature relational development.

When you choose non-acceptance as a bridge to establish your own way, you prejudice this great adventure called life and, in so doing, hinder the ability for it to ever reach its real potential or thrive as it was intended. Diminutive and unfocused development happens in captivity; advantageous growth is also inhibited when Truth is rejected. The person you are dealing with is often robbed of the awareness for the need to change, and is instead blinded by a raised defense to ward off your attempt to control. You also rob yourself of the opportunity to forgive because you, in turn, are blinded by the need to enforce your own way.

Unforgiveness is a blinder; the blocking wall misguidedly erected in an effort to establish self-preservation. Luke 17:33 basically states that those who seek to rescue or deliver themselves from suffering by not facing Truth will end up destroying the very thing they are trying to protect. As Romans 16:17-18 states, we are to *"keep a sharp eye out for those who take bits and pieces of the teaching that you learned and then use them to make trouble or bend the teachings to their own ends. Give these people a wide berth. They have no intention of living for our Lord Jesus Christ. They're only in this for what they can get out of it, and aren't above using pious sweet talk to dupe the unsuspecting"* (MSG). So, if we are encouraged to stay away from those kind of people, it should definitely not be our mission to emulate them! Seeking to control others is the very definition of this type of behavior.

To clarify, we are not referencing acceptance of political agendas or morality driven issues. Make no mistake—God never suggested people are *entitled* to do what they want whenever they want, regardless of the damage to self or others, or anything like that in a broad sense. The Word of God clearly states that everything is *permissible* for us as God's people, but not all things are *beneficial* for us to engage. We are not to be enslaved by anything or brought under its power; just as we are not to allow anything to control us in any way. The point here is to accept a person, as is, and deal with that reality in Truth and with the courage of conviction (1 Corinthians 6:12; Proverbs 11:3 MSG).

To do anything less will only encourage ill will and emotional upheaval on your part toward not only the individual in question, but others as well. Deception on both parts will ensue, propagating confusion while locking down the aspect of oneself specifically intended to navigate life comprehensively and with a giving heart.

For another example, let us consider Jane. She grew up in a Christian home. Her father and mother were married, and she was their only child. Growing up, she was assured of both her parents Love for her. She felt secure in the environment and believed all was wonderful, not perfect, but her life was good. Until her father chose to divorce her mother and leave his family to marry his secretary when Jane was eight. He was an executive whose occupation afforded him the opportunity to travel often.

Jane had very few occasions to see her father following the divorce and often felt neglected and abandoned by him. Jane's father's proclivities overwhelmed and ultimately devastated her because she never came to terms with his desertion. The hurt and pain of rejection careened her into a life of promiscuity and substance abuse, which eventually brought her to a breaking point of emotional torment and physical devastation.

Whether Jane's father's actions could be judged as selfish and callous or reasonable and justified makes no difference. He may also be considered by most to be insensitive, doggish, downright offensive and not worth the skin he's in. The fact remains: *he had a right to his own choices*. He indeed failed to Love, and this failure brought great agony and offense to the family he left behind. In Jane's case, her father's failure to Love was beyond her control and, therefore, *NOT* the cause of her life's destructive path.

This statement might raise your ire and cause all manner of accusations to go through your head. Things like, "But he devastated his family by making a commitment and then breaking it!" or "Even after the divorce, he had a parental obligation to her as his child which he chose to ignore!" These and many more denunciations may be true. However, while Jane's father's failure to Love is stark and obvious, it is Jane's failure to Love that brought about the failings in her own life. She failed to Love by not learning to *accept* her father's choices. It is only through accepting the reality of a circumstance that you are positioned to be able to *deal* with whatever is confronting you in that circumstance. In Jane's case, it was her father's inability to Love.

By facing facts, you can prepare to effectively deal with life. John 8:32 tells us that knowing the Truth will free us; the word "know' here, in Greek, is *ginōskō* (gē-nō'-skō), which means to get a knowledge or understanding of, to perceive or become acquainted with. When we understand and become acquainted with the Truth, we are free from whatever would bind or trip us up outside of the Truth. This makes Truth your shelter and protection. God's Word is Truth, and God is His Word, so when you rest in His Word you are and able to rest in His Truth and be safe (John 1:1; John 17:17; Proverbs 18:10).

Accepting other people's choices and realizing your inability to truly control them by eliminating the prospect of trying to do so, frees you from your part in relational destruction and fortifies you from deep seated hurt. God's Grace is that fortification when you yield to His Word and not your own emotions. Facing issues through the filter of God's Word then becomes paramount to relational success and victory in life. This undoubtedly means walking in forgiveness and, again, this costs you something. It will cost you your pride and your need to have your own way. Choosing forgiveness will initially hurt mainly because of these two reasons.

Hurt birthed through obedience, is the kind of pain for purpose similar to what you get from physical exercise. If you are at all familiar with choosing to get into shape after having neglected your body, you know that when you first began, it felt like untold agony. However, with your commitment to continue on, the pain lessened and as you kept at it, that rocking bod was revealed (or at least a better, healthier one did, right?)! This pain is short-lived and is personally, as well as universally, beneficial.

It is the same with choosing to forgive. As this pain associated with forgiveness means putting down pride and giving up your will, staying out of emotion long enough to choose God's Way is imperative. This pain is a clue to you that the control your flesh had over you is, in effect, dying so God's Spirit may live through you. Forgiveness is another of the multi-facets of Love. It is a tool to freedom, and the more committed you are in employing Love, the more peace you'll have and the stronger you'll become. It is a failure to Love that weakens. On the other hand, the commitment to Love and follow God's Way, is what strengthens.

We are instructed to do our level best to get along with everybody and to *not* insist on getting even because that's *not* our job. God says not to worry because He'll take care of it (Romans 12: 17-19). When we choose unforgiveness (a failure to Love) in a useless effort to protect ourselves from hurt, it's as if we set ourselves in a fighter's stance — arms up to block, feet spread to brace — then tell God, "Get back Big Guy, I got this!" In so doing, we allow an advantage to be gained over us by the devil. This advantage ushers in an onslaught of wrong decisions, which will inevitably culminate in devastating consequences. It's just as 2 Corinthians 2:10-11 in the Amplified Version states:

*If you forgive anyone anything, I too forgive that one; and
what I have forgiven, if I have forgiven anything, has been for
your sake in the presence of and with the approval of Christ,
to keep satan from taking advantage of us; for we are not
ignorant of his schemes.*

The word "advantage" here is *pleonekteō* (ple-o-nek-te'-ō) in
the original Greek text, and it means to have a greater part of or
share in; to gain. In other words, it's as if satan has a hook in you
(like a bridle on a horse) that he can tug on at any time to lead
you to your own demise! This preventable advantage you give
your enemy over you when you hold onto animosity will cost you
much more than it would cost you to humble yourself under the
Mighty Hand of God's Word so He may exalt you through a Spirit
of Forgiveness.

Unforgiveness' lasting consequences will be unavoidably devastating if you allow the enemy, the thief who comes only to steal
your dreams, kill your future, and destroy your purpose, in order to
have this superior position over your life's direction (1 Peter 5:6;
John 10:10). You must face life head on, with eyes open to see victory. Pretending Truth is not Truth will only delay the inevitable.
As the old saying goes, "A hard head makes for a soft behind!" In
the ostrich's case—a buried head gets you a burnt butt! When you
choose to Love, you free yourself; the hooks are removed, and you
are no longer a prisoner to the enemy's wiles. You are removed
from the path that leads to bitterness and wrath, anger and grief
(Ephesians 4:31-32).

Jane failed to Love by choosing not to accept her father as
is and wrongly believing she was justified in judging his actions
and finding him unworthy of forgiveness. She was angry and hurt,
which is very understandable. However, we must live beyond feelings. Remember that Love is choice—not feelings or emotions.
Please remember that God gave us emotions to enhance the journey
of our lives, not set our life's course or destination! We must determine in our minds to entertain Truth over the initial demand to surrender to whatever emotion is at hand (Colossians 3:2).

Giving place to emotion is easier; I know. Just as it's easier to blame the father. After all, it would have been ideal if he'd had the integrity and the strength of character to Love and protect his family as he had promised in his vows. However, even though he chose to forsake his family, the fact of the matter is that Jane has no heaven to put her father in and no hell to send him to. By judging his failure to Love her, she, in turn, failed to Love him. Two negatives adding up positive only work successfully with integers! Two wrongs will never turn out right in real life due to the unpredictable cost and heavy toll the negatives exact spiritually, mentally as well as emotionally. This course of action leads us to our next myth along the destructive path in failing to Love.

Chapter Seven

THE GAME OF BLAME

**"It can make you high, or bring you down, or make you laugh and cry;
it can turn your whole life upside down. If you need a
reason why...blame it on love"**
~ Los Lonely Boys

We live in a world that spins on the axis of falsely blaming Love for most of our interpersonal problems. Besides the short-sighted lack of self-discipline prevalent among our masses, it is also the hot winds of injustice produced when we make others responsible for our own failure to accept them as they are. This is what fuels these relational pitfalls and problems, not Love! It is reprehensible to blame this result on Love when, as stated in the previous chapter, it is actively the *failure* to Love that brings about our difficulties.

Getting involved in the game of blame is inevitable when we have already refused to accept people and situations for who and what they are. Realizing people's limitations, or long-suffering the choices others make, is in no way an approval of or agreement with whatever they choose. On the contrary, this choice is instead a starting point for mediation or intercession. These interventions can open a gateway to obtain peaceful settlements or concrete resolutions.

When we choose the unstable foundation of blaming others for a situation or circumstance, we are automatically setting ourselves up for inhibited growth and ultimate failure. We are also giving the person, around whose neck we are hanging the blame, power over our thoughts and emotions that they were never designed to have and are in no way equipped to handle. We are instead urged to make a clean break with all cutting, backbiting, and profane talk and encouraged to be gentle with one another, sensitive, and forgiving as quickly and thoroughly as God in Christ forgave us (Ephesians 4:31-32).

A failure to Love begins and ends with self because this too is a choice. In an effort to understand an unfortunately forgettable truth, let us borrow the immortal words of Captain Buckaroo Banzai: "No matter where you go, there you are." This phrase is simple, but embodies an exceptionally bold concept. Every condition, state, or circumstance a person finds his or herself in, the one and only common denominator is the *person in* that condition, state, or circumstance. Think about it; every problem you face—be it at home, school, work, church, or any other arena in which people are a factor—the universal component in all those conflicts is *you*. With this in mind, it stands to reason that a major element in the *solution* to the conflict is also you. Instead of assigning blame elsewhere, we must first look to self.

To paraphrase Matthew 7:3-4, it is unwise to worry about a speck in your friend's eye when you have a thousand year-old petrified Redwood in your own. How can you think of saying to your friend, "Let me help you get rid of that speck in your eye," when you can't see past that Redwood in your own eye? We choose to look at others because it is easier to transfer responsibility to others than to take responsibility ourselves. Taking responsibility means bringing *your* time, *your* effort, and *your* commitment into the foundation for the solution, and basically, yes, this will cost you something (refer back to Chapter One).

You are urged to make a careful exploration of who you are, examining your actions, attitudes, and behaviors as well as the work you have been given to do and to concentrate on—no one else's. Don't be impressed with yourself, and don't compare yourself with others. Take responsibility for doing the creative best you can with your own life (Galatians 6:4-5).

This culpable attention to your own actions will leave very little time to assign accountability elsewhere. By doing that useless assigning, you falsely make someone (other than you) answerable, and in your mind, that someone (other than you) must do the work to find the solution. Choosing this phlegmatic course of action not only yields authority to another (an authority God never intended them to have by the way), but it also makes you judge over them by insinuating the person at hand is imperfect, which in turn implies that you are perfect.

When you judge others, you are already condemning yourself (Matthew 7:1). Also, what sense does it make for you to arbitrarily give another imperfect person that kind of misplaced responsibility over your own life?

Our Savior Jesus Christ died on the cross not just to save you from a devil's hell, but also to restore you to an abundant life. Jesus also promised you a Comforter, the Holy Spirit, and said that when He, the Spirit of Truth, comes, He will Guide you into full and complete Truth. You are also promised Power and Ability when the Holy Spirit comes upon you (John 16:13; Acts 1:8 AMP). This power and ability is decreased or greatly dampened when we choose the way opposite of God's Will. To paraphrase Amos 3:3, how can two people walk together without first agreeing on the direction?

Since Jesus promised The Holy Spirit would Guide you into all Truth, it is evident that He Knows the right direction and correct destination. If your course is in direct opposition to God's Will and the prompting of His Spirit (i.e. unforgiveness and judging others), you are not in agreement and, therefore, unable to walk with Him.

According to 2 Peter 1:3-11 in the Amplified, it is by God's Divine Power that you have been given everything you need for living a Godly life. As His child, you have received all of this by coming to know Him, the One Who called you to Himself by means of His Marvelous Glory and Excellence. His Glory and Excellence makes way for His great and precious Promises. These are the promises that enable you to share His Divine Nature, be able to walk in His Love and escape the world's corruption caused by human desires: like holding onto unforgiveness, unresolved anger, bitterness, and strife.

In view of all this, you must make every effort to respond to God's Promises. Supplement your Faith with a generous provision of moral excellence, and moral excellence with knowledge, and knowledge with self-control, and self-control with patient endurance, and patient endurance with godliness, and godliness with brotherly affection, and brotherly affection with Love for everyone (2 Peter 1:5-7 AMP).

The more you grow like this, the more productive and useful you will be in your knowledge of our Lord and Savior Jesus Christ. However, if you fail to develop in this way by refusing to give into Truth, and hold on to your own way, you are allowing yourself to be shortsighted or blind, forgetting that you have been cleansed from your old sins. So, work hard to prove that you really are among those God has called and chosen. Be sure that your conduct signifies and confirms your relationship with God. As you determine in your heart to emulate these qualities, you'll never stumble in your spiritual growth and will live a life that leads others away from the evils of immorality (2 Peter 1:8-10 AMP).

Let's revisit Jane and her father's situation. One major reason Jane went down such a destructive path was not only her unwillingness to forgive, but also her willingness to blame her father for his vicious indifference and lack of care for his family. Yes, according to God's Word, her father was wrong, but again, that was *his* choice. By blaming her father for her life's circumstance, Jane opened the door for even more tragedy to enter her life. Calamities were ushered in on the wake of her anger and bitterness brought about by failing to accept her father's wrong choices, judging him for his behavior, and refusing to follow God's Way of forgiveness.

Please do not take this out of context! Sure, as conceded before, many people do really dumb and selfish things that cause great difficulties and carry devastating consequences, as Jane's father was guilty of causing. However, when Jane judged her father and chose to cage him with unforgiveness, she, in turn, locked the door on her own cage of bitterness!

Only through Christ are we freed from condemnation and are galvanized by the Power of the Holy Spirit Who gives us Life. When Jane turned away from the fountain of God's Empowerment and chose judgment and unforgiveness, she turned away from the very Power to overcome the hurt, pain, and betrayal her father inflicted. It is the flipside of unforgiveness to judge another. This gives the enemy a hook into the soul of the person choosing that method—*every time*! The choice that *feels* justified—unforgiveness—will, in effect, *lead* you away from the very thing that will give you peace—the choice to Love.

This is what caused Jane to falter. Again, choosing to Love is not condoning wrong actions; it is accepting others' free will. When we fail to accept, we open the door to blame. It is a double whammy! Unforgiveness begins first by judging another; this empowers blame, and these destructive choices cause God's Power to be of little to no affect in your life. This debilitating impact limits your life's overall potential. The saying, "God can do anything but fail!" is accurate. However, one thing God **WILL NOT** do is take away your ability to freely choose. He has not changed His Mind on this nor will He withdraw what He has given because the gifts and the calling of God are irrevocable—this includes free will (Mark 7:13; Romans 11:29 AMP).

Deuteronomy 30:19-20 states, God has given you the choice between life and death, between blessings and curses. He calls on heaven and earth to witness the choice you make. He hopes you choose life so that you and your descendants might live! You make this choice by Loving the Lord your God, obeying Him, and committing yourself firmly to Him. This is the key to Life. Not just Life Eternal (heavenly), but Life temporal (earthly).

In Jane's case disobedience means: See Jane be bitter and in so doing; See Jane die a thousand deaths daily. Obedience on the other hand means: See Jane forgive and in turn; See Jane walk in freedom and peace unimaginable. If you Love and obey the Lord, you will have an abundant life. The Bible is also clear on how you show your Love for God. John 14:15 states, "*If you love [God], show it by doing what [He has] told you*" (MSG). Obedience! Obedience to God's Word in regard to showing Love to others is important, but the crucial way to show God you Love Him is by being obedient to Him. This brings us to our next chapter and last point in failing to Love.

Chapter Eight

THE NECESSARY THING

Do you think all God wants are sacrifices—empty rituals just for show? He wants
you to listen to Him! Plain listening is the thing, not staging a lavish religious
production. Not doing what God tells you is far worse than fooling around
in the occult. Getting self-important around God is far worse than
making deals with your dead ancestors. Because you said
No to God's command, He says No to your kingship.
~ 1 Samuel 15:22 MSG

This chapter may seem way off the beaten path, but it is very necessary in the overall accountability for proper impartation concerning Love; it's the principle of Tithes and offerings. You may be asking, "What on earth does Tithes and offerings have to do with Love?" To that, I would again say—Everything! I believe the reason many dismiss Tithes and offerings is because of the profligate communication by some or audacious attacks by others! In spite of this it must be understood that Tithes and offering are an integral part of God's Kingdom because to obey or not to obey directly communicates the abundance of your heart (Matthew 6:21).

As 1 Samuel 15:22 above states, when you say "No!" to God's Command, He says, "No!" to your kingship. It is Kingship or right standing with God, which gives us access to the fullness of His Grace—His Empowerment. Understand, we're not talking about KINship, but KINGship. KINship is your implemented bond with God through the *saving* Power of His Grace; it is yours through the repentance of your sins and the accepting of Christ's Sacrifice.

By doing so, you have not received a spirit that makes you a fearful minion. Instead, you received God's Spirit when He adopted you as His Own Child. This is what many people facetiously refer to as fire insurance to miss hell. KINGship is having the graceful *empowerment* of His unlimitless Power (Romans 8:15-17 AMP, MSG)! There is a difference.

Without His Empowerment, we fall short in our ability to do anything of real and lasting substance; this includes our ability to Love. God confronts us in Malachi 3:10, asking *"Will a man rob God? Yet you are robbing Me! But you say, 'In what way have we robbed You?' In tithes and offerings you have withheld"* (AMP). This is very plain! God takes it personally when you withhold what is His and actually calls it robbery!

He also informs, *"You are cursed with a curse, for you are robbing Me"* (9 AMP). Then, He goes on to command, *"Bring all the tithes (the tenth) into the storehouse [the Church], so that there may be food in My house..."* (10a AMP). There it is. Does this sound like a suggestion? Is God giving a multiple choice? No, He is giving a *Command* with no clauses or interpretations. It is flat-out instruction, and He doesn't leave it there. He goes on to say, *"[Test] Me now in this...if I will not open for you the windows of heaven and pour out for you so great a blessing until there is no more room to receive it"* (10b AMP).

He also Promises to *"rebuke the devourer...for your sake and he will not destroy the fruits of the ground, nor will your vine in the field drop its grapes before harvest. All nations shall call you happy and blessed, for you shall be a land of delight"* (Malachi 3:11-12 AMP). Another translation states, *"God promises to defend you against marauders, protect your wheat fields and vegetable gardens against plunderers"* (11 MSG). This can be translated into modern day as your possessions and the things you value. Well, there it is again! God's Command and Promise concerning Tithes and offerings.

A Heart Issue

Not convinced obeying God's Command to bring your Tithes and give your offerings is a valid one? Are you among those who view this as unimportant or as an archaic concept? Or are you in the all or nothing camp? If you are among the ones that believe if Tithes and offerings are to be recognized from the old testament as still valid, then commands like what God said restricting diet should also apply, all or nothing. The answer to this way of thinking follows the same principle of why we no longer offer up the blood of animals for sin offerings. Jesus, with His Own Blood, entered the Most Holy Place once and secured our redemption forever (Hebrews 9:12). The release from diet restrictions is found in Matthew 15:11 where Jesus clearly states, *"It is not what goes into the mouth of a man that defiles and dishonors him, but what comes out of the mouth, this defiles and dishonors him"* (NLT).

Also, Tithes and offerings have nothing to do with the Law because they were both instituted BEFORE the Law was introduced (Genesis 14:20; Genesis 4:3-5). There is no New Testament scripture that elevates us to a point beyond the fact that God still requires His Tithe and an offering to be brought into His Storehouse. There is no scripture abolishing God's Tithe or shifting It to charities, poor people, widows, orphans, or other individuals or movements involved in "good works." However, Hebrews 7:17 does shift the Priesthood of Melchizedek, a completely mortal priest to Jesus and designate Him Priest forever after the order of Melchizedek!

Abraham brought Tithes to Melchizedek, a priest who, the Scripture says, "lives"—just as we are to continue to bring our "tenth part of all" to our New High Priest, Who was raised to life for us and is in the presence of God at this very moment interceding on our behalf (Hebrews 7:1-2; Romans 8:34 AMP). God is clear! It is an accountability issue, a heart issue; *"for where your treasure is, there your heart, your wishes, your desires; that on which your life centers will be also"* (Matthew 6:21 AMP)!

Still not convinced? Let's examine what God meant by *"You are cursed with a curse, for you are robbing Me"* (Malachi 3:9 AMP). A most horrific description of the results of curses for disobedience is described in the twenty-eighth chapter of Deuteronomy, starting with the sixteenth verse. As a result of disregarding God's Commands, the curse hounds its victims everywhere and in every aspect of life. It tracks them—no matter where they live— inflicting hindrances in sources of revenue, deterioration of health, persecution from enemies, oppression, separation and destruction of families, dissolution into false worship, slow malnourishment, confusion, terror, and eventual madness overtakes them.

This advent of horrific events is not limited to the one under which the curse originated; it can extend to their offspring for generations. These scriptures are Old Testament, but are as vital and relevant for us today as they were then, even though we are now under Grace. Slow down and re-read the manifestations of the curses again. Does it not read like our country's headlines today? While I don't particularly care for statistics, or the way one can always find the numbers needed to bolster their point, there are still thousands of articles out there that illustrate the terrible repercussions imposed by the curse mentioned in Scripture. I'll just put the first article to come up in my search engine for an example to illustrate the point designation cited concerning the curse besetting those who ignore God's Word:

Sources of Revenue Hindered: A November 16th, 2017 issue of WSWS.org sported an article written by Jessica Goldstein stating that "millions of workers in the US face a life of part-time, precarious employment". Goldstein goes on to note, "The Bureau of Labor Statistics monthly job report for October 2017 released on November 3 revealed that staggering 4.8 million American workers are stuck working in part-time, precarious positions when they would prefer full time work, referred to officially as "involuntary part-time workers." Involuntary part-time workers often must piece together two or more jobs just to make ends meet. Often, these jobs are low wage and do not offer benefits. If they do, the benefits they offer are out of reach financially for many workers. This type of life leaves many workers mentally and physically exhausted. Rushing from one job to the next, often outside of normal hours, leaves little time for family life, leisure, education, or even the ability to look for a better job."

Deterioration of Health: Thomson Reuters posted on October 4th, 2017 on CBC.ca an article which stated, "according to the CDC, 40% of cancers diagnosed in US are related to Obesity."

Reuters goes on to write, "The rates of 12 obesity-related cancers rose by 7% from 2005 to 2014, an increase that is threatening to reverse progress in reducing the rate of cancer in the United States, U.S. health officials say."

Persecution from Enemies: Updated December 18th, 2017 on CNN.com, an article entitled, *US Terrorist Attacks Fast Facts,* lists several terrorist attacks on US soil from the year 1978 to 2017, one of which was on October 31st, 2017 – "Eight people are killed and almost a dozen injured when a 29-year-old man in a rented pickup truck drives down a busy bicycle path near the World Trade Center in New York. The suspect has been identified as Sayfullo Habibullaevic Saipov. Authorities found a note near the truck used in the incident, claiming the attack was made in the name of ISIS, a senior law enforcement official said."

Oppression: A Washingtonpost.com article entitled, *Senate hearing examines free speech on college campuses after incidents at UC-Berkeley, Middlebury*, written by Sarah Larimer, was about a free speech protest in Civic Center Park in Berkeley, California. "U.S. senators focused Tuesday on the issues surrounding free speech on college campuses, as some expressed concerns that voices have been suppressed because they have been deemed offensive, and others raised questions about how to balance First Amendment rights with safety. There is no point in having a student body on campus if competing ideas are not exchanged and analyzed and respected by each other," said Sen. Charles E. Grassley (R-Iowa), chairman of the Senate Judiciary Committee. The committee examined the issue at a Tuesday hearing titled "Free Speech 101: The Assault on the First Amendment on College Campuses.'"

Separation and Destruction of Families: An article on APA.org adapted from the *Encyclopedia of Psychology, Volume 8*; Alan E. Kazdin, PhD, Editor-in-Chief stated, "Marriage and divorce are both common experiences. In Western cultures, more than 90 percent of people marry by age 50. Healthy marriages are good for couple's mental and physical health. They are also good for children; growing up in a happy home protects children from mental, physical, educational and social problems. However, about 40 to 50 percent of married couples in the United States divorce. The divorce rate for subsequent marriages is even higher."

Dissolution into False Worship: "What are some modern forms of idolatry (false worship)?" The answer found on GotQuestions. org adapted from *No Gods But God: Confronting Our Modern-Day Idolatry* by Dennis Newkirk: "All the various forms of modern idolatry have one thing at their core: self. We no longer bow down to idols and images. Instead we worship at the altar of the god of self. This brand of modern idolatry takes various forms. First, we worship at the altar of materialism, which feeds our need to build our egos through the acquisition of more "stuff." Our homes are filled with all manner of possessions. We build bigger and bigger houses with more closets and storage space in order to house all the things we buy, much of which we haven't even paid for yet. Most of our stuff has "planned obsolescence" built into it, making it useless in no time, and so we consign it to the garage or other storage space. Then we rush out to buy the newest item, garment or gadget and the whole process starts over. This insatiable desire for more, better, and newer stuff is nothing more than covetousness. The tenth commandment tells us not to fall victim to coveting; *You shall not covet your neighbor's house. You shall not covet your neighbor's wife, or his manservant or maidservant, his ox or donkey, or anything that belongs to your neighbor* (Exodus 20:17). God doesn't just want to rain on the parade of our buying sprees. He knows we will never be happy indulging our materialistic desires because it is satan's trap to keep our focus on ourselves and not on Him."

Slow Malnourishment: Andrew Soergel, Economy Reporter posted, December 7th, 2015 on UsNews.com. "There's been little improvement in the country's food accessibility in recent years, and that's bad news for millions of Americans. America's top 75 food retailers – led by Wal-Mart, Kroger, Costco, Target and Safeway – opened more than 10,000 new locations between

2011 and the first quarter of 2015, according to an analysis published Monday by The Associated Press. But when the AP stripped away convenience stores and dollar stores that don't usually provide fresh meal options, it found that only a little over 250 new supermarkets cropped up in the country's expansive food deserts, which held more than 18 million U.S. citizens as of 2010, according to the U.S. Department of Agriculture. Federal agencies define a food desert as a community that doesn't have sufficient access to fresh, healthy and affordable food – typically provided by a supermarket or grocery store. At least 500 people or 33 percent of a region's population must live more than a mile from the nearest supermarket or grocery store for census tracts to be considered food deserts. For non-metro regions, that distance benchmark is extended to 10 miles."

Confusion, terror and eventual madness overtake them: Wikipedia details the 2017 Las Vegas shooting. "On the night of Sunday, October 1st, 2017, a gunman opened fire on a crowd of concertgoers at the Route 91 Harvest music festival on the Las Vegas Strip in Nevada, leaving 58 people dead and 546 injured. Between 10:05 and 10:15 p.m. PDT, 64-year-old Stephen Paddock of Mesquite, Nevada, fired more than 1,100 rounds from his suite on the 32nd floor of the nearby Mandalay Bay hotel. About an hour after Paddock fired his last shot into the crowd of 22,000, he was found dead in his room from a self-inflicted gunshot wound. His motive is unknown. The incident is the deadliest mass shooting committed by an individual in the United States."

These examples are broad and not restricted to the time in which we live, but pointedly shed light on the issue. Whether you are reading this now or years after its first publishing, as long as disobedience to God's Law reigns, the curse will rear its regrettable head. It could also be argued that the people involved in the cited examples were not Christians, so I ask you to examine your own life as a Believer. If you are bringing the Tithe and giving an offering, is your life blessed, are you on get-by street or is your circumstance improving? If you are in disobedience, how is your life holding up? Do you see any reminders of the curse reverberating throughout your life?

If you are an individual whose economic standing far surpasses the norm, do you have peace, are you in excellent health? Is your family whole, your spouse and your children at peace with you? I'm not suggesting your life will be perfect if you are obedient to God; it won't be. Psalm 34:19 states, "*Many hardships and perplexing circumstances confront the righteous, but the Lord rescues him from them all*" (AMP). Are you being rescued? Be honest and if you haven't been—then be obedient. God has not changed His Mind. He Is, and will remain the same today as He was yesterday and as He will be forever (Hebrews 13:8).

If you are deliberately disobedient in the face of God's Directives, God says, "*I am GOD—yes, I AM. I haven't changed. And because I haven't changed, [you] haven't been destroyed. You have a long history of ignoring my commands. You haven't done a thing I've told you. Return to me so I can return to you*" (Malachi 3:6-7 MSG).

The Love Connection

Keep in mind that all Scripture is God-breathed, given by divine inspiration, and is profitable for instruction, for conviction of sin, for correction of error and restoration to obedience, and for training in righteousness, as in learning to live in conformity to God's Will, both openly and surreptitiously. God's Word will strengthen you to behave honorably with personal integrity and moral courage so that you, the person of God, may be complete and proficient as well as outfitted and thoroughly equipped for every good work (2 Timothy 3:16-17 AMP).

Learning to Love will equip God's Saints! The Empowerment of God is essential to the advancement of His Saints in every area of life and ministry. Tithes and offerings are qualifying keys to the trove of God's abounding riches rooted in the ability to Love! Repenting and accepting God's Grace brings you into God's Family, which makes you His Child and therefore, His Heir. This makes you a joint heir with Christ, sharing His Spiritual Blessing and Inheritance (Romans 8:17). As an heir, you are *entitled* to share all spiritual blessings and inheritance. However, being obedient to His command to bring your Tithe and give your offering *qualifies* you to receive the *fullness* of these blessings and inheritance.

I'm not talking about Salvation. That is secured for you through Christ. No, I'm talking about KINGship. To bring perspective, think of a wealthy father who sets up trust funds for all his children. Being an heir of this wealthy man entitles each child to their respective trust. However, the qualifying factor is that they must wait until they each reach twenty-one years of age to be *eligible* for their personally entitled funds to be released. As twenty-one years of age is the qualifying factor in this trust fund example, Tithes and offerings are qualifying factors to acquiring the *full* provision of God's inheritance.

This may sound like a farfetched idea, but God states plainly in the Amplified of Malachi 3:10 to prove Him in this. Be aware that if you refuse to be obedient, someone else will choose obedience and gain the fullness of the blessing as God meant for you to receive. When this happens, don't get mad, get right! Repent and be obedient! You have a lot to lose in disobedience and everything to gain in being obedient.

So, try Him—but don't get it twisted. You are in no way buying your way into God's Good Graces. God is not an extortionist, nor is He in the protection racket. Yes, you want and need His Favor, but He does *not* need or *want* your money. It's not about that for Him; it's about the state of your heart. The place where your treasure is, is the place you will most want to be, and end up being (Matthew 6:21 MSG). He wants you *with* Him and He makes it *your* choice. Being obedient shows your trust and Love for God.

Love is a *Spiritual* inheritance. Disqualification through disobedience limits Love's Spiritual authorization because of the curse. 1 Corinthians 6:9-10 reads, "*Don't you realize that those who do wrong will not inherit the Kingdom of God? Don't fool yourselves. Those who indulge in sexual sin, or who worship idols, or commit adultery, or are male prostitutes, or practice homosexuality, or are [thieves], or [greedy people], or drunkards, or are abusive,* *or [cheat] people—none of these will inherit the [**Kingdom of God**]"* (NLT).

The Kingdom of God, in Greek, is *basileia* (bä-sē-lā'-ä) / *theos* (the-o's), and it refers to the royal power, kingship, and dominion over the things of God. The Kingdom of *God* is not to be confused with the actual Kingdom of *Heaven* where God dwells (Matthew 18:1), but rather the right or authority to rule in this present world (more on this in Chapter Seventeen). Disobedience to God's Word in an area places you *under* the curse in *that* area.

Obedience to God's avenue of blessing is better than sacrificing His Favor on the altar of your own selfish pride and fear of not having enough. This is counterproductive and lacks Faith in God's Promise of Provision. The place where God provided a ram as a sacrifice, Abraham named Jehovah Jireh, which means the Lord Will Provide (Genesis 22:14 AMP). To this day, Christians still use that Name. Why? Because God faithfully promised to do abundantly more than all we could ever dare ask or think, which will go infinitely beyond our greatest prayers, hopes, and dreams, according to His Power that is at work within us (Ephesians 3:20 AMP).

Food For Thought

As a child of God, you are like any wealthy heir. If you reside in the home (the Word) of your wealthy Father, you will reap daily benefits as a part of His household (KINship). However, your access to the full portfolio of God's Endowment (KINGship) toward you will be limited to you, if you continue to *willingly* refuse God by denying Him **HIS** Tithe and your offering. Giving dues, or whatever your sect of Believers deems a reasonable compensation instead of what is required by God, will limit the Power of your own faith's potential due to the dampening of God's Enablement in your life because of willful disobedience.

Besides, Matthew 6:21 is quite clear, *"for where your treasure is, there your heart, your wishes, your desires; that on which your life centers will be also"* (AMP). The bottom line is this: obedience to bring Tithes and to give offerings is a statement to God that you trust Him, while disobedience means you don't. It is that simple. If you are not yet convinced, it is my prayer that God deals with your heart so you can let go of what's not yours to hold onto anyway, and grab on to God's Promise to provide for you. Tithes and offering support the marshaling in of this Promise and if you are still dismissive of this command or are on that proverbial fence, one main reason is because it is...

Chapter Nine

A MATTER OF FAITH

Without faith it is impossible to please Him:
for he that cometh to God must believe that
He is, and that He is a rewarder of them
that diligently seek him
~ Hebrews 11:6

If you are familiar with Hebrews 11:6, have you ever pondered why it's without *Faith* and not something else, such as forgiveness, kindness, sorrow for wrongdoing, Hope, or even Love, that makes it impossible to please God? Well, I did, so I petitioned God about it and He blew my mind with His answer. You see, due to the fact that we are made after the Image and Likeness of God, forgiveness, kindness, remorse, hope, and love all have an expected residue within the human condition in varying degrees.

It is *only* Faith that comes *directly from* God. We can forgive, show kindness, be contrite, have hope for tomorrow, and love others in our own finite understanding. However, only God can give the measure of Faith. It too, because of Grace, is a Gift from God. You may not agree with this statement, because mainstream has professed faith as if it is a key to the city, unlocking everything conceivable. George Michael even informed us back in the 80s that we have to have "faith, a faith, a faithaaa!"

So give me a minute here to explain. You see, we confuse Faith with strong or sincere belief. We make them synonymous or interchangeable when, according to God, they are not. Belief is a naturally accruing condition brought about through observation, persuasion, and external familiarization. According to Webster, the definition of belief is a confidence in the truth or existence of something not immediately susceptible to rigorous proof. This basically means having an opinion on something or having a confidence in something that may or may not be based in Truth.

Romans 10:9 reads, *"If thou shalt confess with thy mouth the Lord Jesus, and shalt believe in thine heart that God hath raised him from the dead, thou shalt be saved."* The word believe, in Greek, is *pisteuō (pē-styü'-ō), which* means to think to be true, to be persuaded of, to credit or place confidence in. This also speaks of opinion based on what is thought to be truth, not what is definitively true.

Now, let's take a look at Faith. Hebrews 11:1 reads, *"Now faith is the substance of things hoped for, the evidence of things not seen."* Faith, in Greek, is *pistis (pē'-stēs)*, which means conviction of the Truth of anything, belief. Pistis' definition *encompasses* belief, whereas pisteuō's definition does not mention Faith or the conviction of Truth; it is *only* belief. This stands to reason that Faith (*pistis*) has more to it than just belief.

Going back to Romans 10:9, the reason belief, and not Faith, is mentioned for Salvation to be obtained is because when we were sinners we were not able to access Faith in our sinful state. The only force to accompany reason at our disposal was belief. Just like reason, it is a human derivative that pales in comparison to God Given Faith. It is only *after* Salvation that Faith is then attainable because it is a Gift only accessed through God's Grace, by accepting Jesus as our Savior.

Hebrews 12:2 admonishes us to focus on Jesus because *He* is the Author, Initiator, and Perfecter of our Faith (*pistis*). Romans 12:3 states in The New American Standard Bible that *"God has allotted to each a measure of faith"* (*pistis*). Each mentioned in this verse concerns Believers because the natural, unbelieving man does not accept the teachings and revelations of the Spirit of God found in the Word of God. God-filled instructions are absurd and illogical to the natural mind, rendering it incapable of being understood because Godly directives can only be Spiritually discerned and appreciated (1 Corinthians 2:14).

Note that there is a bridge between belief and Faith; it's called Hope. God, in His Eternal Plan, chose to make known to you the Gospel of Christ so that you might believe. When you did, by accepting Jesus as Savior, the Grace of God gave you the Hope of Glory, the guarantee of the fullness of God's Power. It is BELIEF that saves and HOPE that inspires, but it is FAITH that makes us more than conquerors (Colossians 1:27; Romans 8:37-38 AMP)!

The "measure" mentioned in Romans is an initial endowment and can be increased exponentially according to Romans 10:17 in The Amplified, which reads, *"So faith comes from hearing what is told, and what is heard comes by the preaching of the message concerning Christ."* I believe this is one of the many reasons we are encouraged to diligently study the Word (2 Timothy 2:15). As mentioned in earlier chapters, the Word of God is the Power of God that saves us and imparts the knowledge of the Grace of God that empowers us! Now, it is revealed that the Word also quantifies Faith (Romans 1:16, 2 Timothy 2:1, Romans 10:17)! So then how are all of these wonderful and extraordinarily beneficial blessings derived from hearing and studying the message concerning Christ?

The Apostle John reveals this great mystery to us in the first chapter of his Gospel when he proclaims, *"In the beginning, before all time was the Word (Christ), and the Word was with God, and the Word was God Himself. He was continually existing in the beginning, co-eternally with God. All things were made and came into existence through Him; and without Him not even one thing was made that has come into being. In Him was life and the power to bestow life, and the life was the Light of men"* (John 1:1-4 AMP).

Wow! How Awesome is that? The Bible we carry around, google scriptures from, and lay nonchalantly on our coffee tables is Alive and Powerful. It was also made Flesh and Blood and lived among us in the person of Jesus Christ (John 1:14). Proverbs 30:5 reads, *"Every word of God is pure; [He] is a shield to those who put their trust in [Him]"* (NKJV). The wording is very significant here. It does not read, *it* is a shield, but *HE* is a shield. God *Is* His Word.

Have you figured out yet why it is impossible to please God without Faith? As just revealed, God *Is* His Word and the only way to increase Faith is by hearing and studying God's Word. With this in mind, it would stand to reason, the more time you spend in the Word, the more time you are spending with God Himself! Doesn't it please you when those you Love spend quality time with you? When they devote energy, effort, and show genuine affection toward you—doesn't this please you as well? Wouldn't you then want to reward them?

Hebrews 11:6 says it all, *"But without faith it is impossible to please Him, for he who comes to God must believe that He is, and that He is a rewarder of those who diligently seek Him"* (NKJV). What is this reward? MORE FAITH! Remember Faith in Greek means conviction of the truth. Where does that conviction come from? From God, of course, by His Son Jesus Christ through the impartation of the Holy Spirit!

Belief alone is mere supposition. It is guesswork based on a conglomeration of ideas your psyche has found palatable, acceptable, or critical to the propagation of your *own* convictions. Your belief in the Truth, coupled with God's stamp of agreement on that Truth, moves you past your own regulated understanding into the Power of God's Own Faith. The Conviction of Truth! The Faith of the Son of God is yours because of His Strength and not your own. It is His Strength effectively working in you, energizing you and giving you the desire and the ability to do what pleases Him (Galatians 2:20; Philippians 2:13 AMP).

The more Faith we have, the more God is pleased. The Bible declares that Faith is the Power that works in us to receive from God, makes all things possible through Grace, and empowers us to fulfill our destiny. More accurately, it is Faith that grants us access to God's Unlimited Power (Ephesians 3:20, Matthew 17:20, Romans 5:2)! Faith is, as Jimmy Walker is famous for saying—Di-no-mite!

Faith is the catalyst to receiving all God has for you as well as the key element that enables you to have confidence in God's Love for you. As a Loving Parent, He's pleased when you are assured of His Love and are equipped with what you need to receive the Abundant Life He's Promised you. This is why you are reminded in several scriptures to live by Faith, walking every day of your life framed by the working of Faith. No matter how small Faith may be in you at this point, it can still move mountains (Romans

1:17, Matthew 17:20). The mountain moving properties of Faith, as applied to Love, are very crucial to the development of your ability to walk in Love.

It all goes hand in hand. For in Christ, your most conscientious religious convictions, or lack thereof, don't amount to anything. What really matters is the real you on the inside, which manifests through Faith empowered by Love (Galatians 5:6). This is a threefold cord not easily broken. Ecclesiastes 4:12 states, "*A person standing alone can be attacked and defeated, but two can stand back-to-back and conquer. Three are even better, for a triple-braided cord is not easily broken*" (MSG). Grace authorizes the expectation Hope releases for Love to flow freely, and Faith is the framework through which Love is communicated. Faith, Hope, and Love, a threefold cord not easily broken!

However, when the framework of Faith has not been established appropriately, nothing of substance or stability is available to guide or sustain you on the path of Love. Think of a coloring book. The pictures are a framework we then color—hopefully—inside the lines. If you have a blank page and crayons but no concept of what a picture is, you'll have no "framework" reference in which to outline or frame a picture. Without such framework or knowledge, you'll be reduced to scribbling indiscriminately on the blank page.

This is what we do in our relationships without the framework of Faith derived from God's Word. We indiscriminately wander aimlessly throughout our lives, stumbling from one person to the next without focus or vision, damaging lives and being damaged in return. We have gone into captivity to our own selfish and misguided desires due to lack of knowledge found in God's Word. His Word "frames" the purpose for each and every one of our lives (Isaiah 5:13).

Another reason it is impossible to please God without Faith is because Faith is the framework through which God can move effectively in the lives of Believers. Again, Love fills the framework of Faith. Without Faith in place, it is difficult for God to move effectively in the lives of His children or for His children to be effective in showing Love one to another, let alone being able to effectively spread His Gospel to this dying world.

The Journey

At this point, I am optimistic that you are convinced of three key foundational Truths. First, the Bible is the infallible Word of the Most High God. He means exactly what He has said in His Word. What He says goes, and it is not up for debate because His Powerful Word is alive and sharp as a surgeon's scalpel, cutting through everything, whether doubt or defense, and laying us open to listen, yield and obey (Hebrews 4:12). Nothing and no one is impervious to or exempted from God's Word. Romans 14:12 admonishes that each of us will give our own personal account to God.

We can't get away from it, no matter what. The Word of God is like a sledgehammer busting a rock, yet at the same time It brings light and gives understanding to the ordinary. Within Its pages resides God's Power, and It is a Seed that (when planted) yields fruit to judge the poor, decides with equity for the meek of the earth, and will destroy the wicked (Jeremiah 23:29; Psalm 119:130, Romans 1:16, Luke 8:11)!

Heaven and earth shall pass away, but God proclaims that His Word will never pass away. God's Word is our Standard as Believers, A Rock of Ages, and upon this Rock we are to build our lives so the enemy of our souls will not conquer us (Isaiah 11:4, Matthew 24:35 AMP; Matthew 16:18 NLT)!

Second, God is Love, and because of this, Love transcends human effort and transforms the human heart. Love is the catalyst for change! This change begins with the selfless determination to tread daily within the boundaries of God's Grace. The Grace of God imparts the Hope of Glory. I pray that God, the source of Hope, will fill you completely with Joy and Peace because you trust in Him. As this unfolds, you will overflow with confident Hope through the Power of the Holy Spirit. Yielding to these factors will give you the ability to accept yourself and others as is, as well as condition you to refuse to get involved in the game of blame.

Personal responsibility for your life's course, as well as operating in obedience to God's Directives, will be your life's focus when you choose to Love. A Love Walk will impart direction and purpose! Knowing the Truth of God's Word is the very fuel of

Love's interpersonal design. God is the Power to Love's exchange! You cannot reach the height of Love's potential without God's Empowerment or Direction. Without God, love is limited. With God, Love is limitless (Galatians 5:16, Colossians 1:27, Romans 15:13).

The third and final point I hope resonates within you is that Faith is essential to the galvanization of your eternal walk with God. It is the building block and bridge to all God has for you and all God wants to do through you. Remember always, it is Hope that authorizes the flow of Love and Faith is the framework through which Love is transferred. These are the highlights of Grace's impartation to you as a Believer.

Faith is the abiding trust in God and His Promises. Hope is the confident expectation of Eternal Salvation and God's divine earthly intervention. Love is the unselfish charity for others growing out of God's Love for you! The Bible goes on to enumerate that of these three, the greatest is Love (1 Corinthians 13:13). It is the greatest because God is Love. He is Love's Source, so Love cannot fail.

In the next few chapters, we will address the framework of Love's impartation through Faith concerning the Family. The Family Unit is the foundation of civilized society as well as the structure God designed to be a bearer and dispatcher of Love here on earth. Hearing is what inspires belief, but hearing Truth is what builds the framework of Faith. The foundation of the actions that convey Love is taught. The tenants of Faith, detailed and outlined in God's Word, produce actions that express Love. Heeding these directives will strengthen your walk with God, and the new, emerging sense of direction will empower your life's purpose. As you find your purpose, you'll be able to fix your focus and allow Love to fill the essential components in your heart in order to have a fulfilled life.

Your very existence will be a letter that anyone can read, not with ink, but with God's Living Spirit. By just looking at you, all will know that Christ Himself is writing the letter of your life (2 Corinthians 3:2,3 MSG). Words frame Faith, and Faith is fulfilled through Love. God has set up the Family Dynamic within His Word. As we go forward to navigate the maze of His inspired direction, keep in mind that there is an agenda to Love: certain parameters are God ordained, sanctioned, and consecrated for the sole purpose of navigation through the web of life's challenges.

Many hardships and perplexing circumstances do and will continue to confront you as a Believer. When you remain in Christ by studying and following His Word, remaining vitally united with Him and allowing His Message to live in your heart, you can ask whatever you wish and it will be done for you. The Lord will rescue you from all troubles. If not physically, He will rescue you emotionally and mentally (John 15:7, Psalm 34:19, Philippians 4:7, John 16:33). Like coloring inside the lines of an already established picture, only God's Design will properly build the framework of Family. Only through Faith will that framework fill and stay full with His Love.

ATTENTION

Getting wisdom is the wisest thing you can do!
And whatever else you do,
develop good judgment.
~ Proverbs 4:7 (NLT)

Before we journey any further with Family, this must be clarified. Under no circumstance are you to draw from these next chapters that physical or emotional abuse is to be tolerated or ignored. Everything to follow is in light of the understanding that abuse is wrong and in no way, shape, fashion, or form does God promote it or excuse it toward the wife, children, or husband.

If you are in an abusive situation, please understand that the abuse is not your fault. Again—you are not at fault! Also be aware, cessation of an abuser's debasement will not be accomplished by your "being good" nor with the addition of perceived perfection.

The deficiency lies in the heart of the abuser. The only way to resolve abuse is to expose it. So I encourage you to seek help. Seek it now or at the safest opportunity—at all cost! To not do so could cost you your life or the lives of those you Love. It is true that God's Grace is sufficient! However, to disregard good judgment is not wise. Seek help!

A family member of mine explained the necessity of having to divorce her husband when he would not see reason or see the need for changing his physically abusive ways. She did so, very eloquently with this one statement, "He would not have meant to kill me, but I would not have been any less dead." I'm sure she wasn't the first to say that phrase, but it is nonetheless very applicable to the imperative of getting away from an abusive, irreconcilable situation post haste!

With this understood, the information in the chapters to follow are not "cookie cutter" resolutions to the problems you may be facing, nor do they advise on how to rectify your situation overnight. The guiding principles found within the pages of God's Word are to shed light on the darkened spaces of misunderstanding or obliviousness you may have been taught or inadvertently acquired concerning His Original Design for Family and dealings with people in general.

We are sanctified and liberated by the Truth of God's Word. The more Word you have, the more Truth you have. The more Truth you have, the freer you are. Whom the Son has made free, is free without question (John 8:36, 32; John 17:17).

Chapter Ten

ALL FOR ONE AND ONE FOR ALL!

"Family quarrels are bitter things. They don't go according to any rules.
They're not like aches or wounds, they're more like splits in the skin that
won't heal because there's not enough material."
~ F. Scott Fitzgerald

Have you ever wondered why there were Three Musketeers (Athos, Porthos, and Aramis)? Young d'Artagnan tagged along to make four, but the original was three. Three is the magic number according to our School House Rock friends as well. Why? The Trinity, of course! It is true; nowhere in the Bible is "Trinity" found. Paul Kroll addresses this in an article on Grace Communion International's website, "Some people who reject the Trinity doctrine claim that the word 'Trinity' is not found in Scripture. Of course, there is no verse that says, 'God is three Persons' or 'God is a Trinity.' This is evident and true, but it proves nothing. There are many words and phrases that Christians use, but are nevertheless not found in the Bible. For example, the word 'Bible' is not found in the Bible." I simply love that quote!

Although the word "Trinity" is not found *in* scripture, scripture definitively proclaims the Trinitarian view of God's Nature. One such scripture is Matthew 28:19, which admonishes Believers to, *"Go ye therefore, and teach all nations, baptizing them in the name of the [**Father**], and of the [**Son**], and of the [**Holy Ghost**]."* God's Triune Nature is also revealed in us, for we have a ***spirit***, we are a ***soul,*** and we live in a ***body*** (1 Thessalonians 5:23). Many things in nature, as well as things manufactured, reflect this trinitarian theme.

It seems inescapable. This I believe, is also true concerning Family. It is not by accident or coincidence, but by Design!

God's divine order for family is reflected in the fifth chapter of Ephesians. The whole chapter teems with substantive reflection on bettering society through proper individual actions and specific methods to support and fortify familial bonds. God the Father, as the "Head" of the Trinity, sent Christ to us to save us and refers to God the Son, Jesus, as Son. I believe this illustrates conclusively that God the Father is Head Honcho (John 3:17).

This is clearly the Father's role in a family as reflected in Ephesians 5:23 which reads *"For the husband is the head of the wife, even as Christ is the head of the church."* God the Holy Spirit is described as the Comforter, sent by the Father Who teaches all things and brings all things to our remembrance (John 14:26). Sounds like Mom to me; and as already mentioned, we have God the Son in the Person of Jesus Christ.

According to John 1:18, He is the only begotten son. Begotten is the past participle of beget, which means to bring a child into existence by the process of reproduction. Luke 2:52 states that Jesus *grew* in stature and wisdom—something every parent hopes their own children accomplish! Stature, in this verse, is a measurement of time, a term for length of life. Father, Mother, Child—three-in-one family.

The chief reason the Family is under attack by the enemy is because Family is a trinitarian framework established by God for the dispersal of Love here on earth! The Family, by God's Design, was instituted to promote unity, support growth, and empower long and healthy lives (Amos 3:3, Proverbs 22:6, Ephesians 6:4, Exodus 20:12).

Helen Keller boldly stated, "The only thing worse than blindness is having sight with no vision." Having a family without any idea of its purpose is having sight with no vision. Each element encompassing a family unit has its own designation, function, and purpose. This is why the reassigning of these roles has been on the societal agenda for decades. God is not the author of confusion, but of peace (1Corinthians 14:33).

Morality, ethics, and good character cannot be legislated or fostered through the rule of law. Which is why laws are repeatedly broken and need frequent enforcement. No, morality, ethics, and good character are fueled by righteousness, an internal implementation not an external lever. They were meant to be homegrown and Love spun. This is what God designed family to impart. Family was instituted to perfect the imperfections and pitfalls of human development in a safe, stable environment free from criticism, judgment, and rejection. A God-centered Family will produce God-centered and, therefore, moral and ethical children, graced with good character. Note here, *God-centered* and NOT RELIGIOUS, because God is not religious, He is Holy (1 Peter 1:16, Leviticus 11:44, 45).

Family was also designed as a permanent arrangement. Mark 10:9 reads, "*What therefore God hath joined together, let not man put asunder.*" Asunder is *chorizo* (khō-rē'-zō) in Greek and means to divide, to separate one's self from, to depart. The Amplified version reads, "*Therefore, what God has united and joined together, man must not separate by divorce.*" What causes this to happen? I'm sure several reasons come to mind from adultery, to financial problems, to The Spell of the Blue Angel!

The Blue Angel Spell sounded so quirky when I first heard it, so I just had to look it up. According to an article on DivorceMag. com, the poet W.H. Auden believed "people get divorced when they discover, to their shock, that they have married an ordinary human being—flawed and boring—and not an Isolde or Tristan—the ideal lovers of mythology. Or, like Don Juan, they can only approach but never attain perfection through a multitude of lovers. In either case, it's our attraction to the bright flame of the absolute that destroys us like moths." Basically, the "spell" is broken with the onslaught of reality.

Whatever reason we want to attribute to this diabolical undermining of the ability to make common-sense decisions, all roots stem from the inability to Love as God Loves due to a lack of knowledge *of* His Word or a lack of Faith *in* His Word!

Your belief in the truth regarding what the Bible says is Truth concerning marriage, coupled with God's stamp of agreement on that Truth, moves you past your own regulated understanding into the Power of God's Own Faith (Galatians 2:20). The Faith of the Son of God is yours! His Faith is yours to have. That includes Faith in marriage, as well as Faith in what marriage stands for, because His Strength and not your own is effectively working in you, energizing you, and giving you the desire and the ability to do what is pleasing to Him concerning Family. This will happen only when you have made up your mind that God's Way alone reigns supreme. All you have to do is *yield* to His Way, not your own. Remember, God is for you! He wants what is best for you.

John 15:12 states, *"This is My commandment, that you love and unselfishly seek the best for one another, just as I have loved you"* (AMP). Love here is *agapaō* (ä-gä-pä›-ō) in Greek. It has to do with affection springing from the choice to Love and means to welcome, entertain, be fond of, well pleased, and contented with. Please take note *agapaō*, a derivative of *agapē* (God's Love) is the word used and not *philia* (brotherly), *storge* (familial) or even *eros* (romantic). This is very significant in translation. This denotes God's Presence in the command to Love. *He will do it through you!*

In everything you do you are to know, acknowledge, recognize, and trust God. As you *yield* to Him, He will make your paths straight and smooth (Proverbs 3:6 AMP). He'll remove obstacles that block your way or strengthen you to stand when you have been obedient to His Word concerning His Standard to Love. His Standard is the only one that counts because He is Love's Origin. *All* parts of the Family are *for one* goal—Love. *And one* Family unit *for all* the world to see emulate God's Perfect Plan—to Love. *All for one and one for all!*

The Ties that Bind

Ephesians is crowded with functional reflection on suitable and specific commands to support and fortify familial ties. Chapter three of this book focused on erroneously accrediting emotional interpretations as Love, to bring clarity to why we have such false views in the application of Love. This unilateral fallacy is why we have an abundance of the train wrecks we call families! Yes, train wrecks.

Please don't take offense if you happen to come from an ideal, lovingly supportive, and thriving family that's free from strife, division, and bankrupt ideals. I am genuinely happy for you if you came from such a model situation, but for the rest of us who have not, to which our Therapist's money lines pockets, and the teaming cells of our nation's jails will attest, let us take the time to delve closer into *God's* Idea of Family. You only have to look around at the fallout and devastation of our collective choices being played out in our society and the entire world to see that our way seems to not be working out so well.

The husband is tasked to Love his wife as Christ Loves the Church. The wife is to submit unto her own husband as unto the Lord. The children are to obey and honor their Father and Mother, so their lives will go well and their days will be long upon the earth (Ephesians 5:25, 22, Ephesians 6:1-3). These tasks are not so naturally executed. Mistakes, as well as deliberate missteps, will occur. However, God intended for the surety, continued strength, and stability of the Family to get us through it all.

A Family, above all, is meant to have a fervent and unfailing Love for one another, because Love covers a multitude of sins! Love overlooks unkindness and selflessly seeks the best for others (1 Peter 4:8). Unfortunately, due to our past ignorance in the area of Love, it is the Family or lack thereof that causes the breakdown of forward constructive, cohesive development. Another of my most sincere prayers is, as President Truman stated, "The buck stops here!"

The popular definition of buck passing, or passing the buck, is the act of attributing one's own responsibility to another person or group. Each person's individual choice makes up the ever-expanding product of the whole. If your choices thus far are working for you, and you have a full and complete life free from doubt, worry, or discord, you may not be interested in the pages to follow.

However, if you are seeking more than what you are experiencing in the area of fulfillment in your life, if you want the assured freedom promised in God's Word to permeate your soul and unleashed Joy to overflow your spirit, please soldier on.

The following chapters outline God's Design for a Wife, Husband, and Parent as well as a single individual in the matters of life and of Love. His Plan is for your good. Today is the first day of the rest of your life. Make your choices from here on out matter! Live on purpose, and side with God. Choose to do it His Way. His Way Leads to Life Everlasting and Eternal Joy (Matthew 25:46, John 17:13).

Chapter Eleven

FIT HELP

Now the Lord God said, "It is not good (beneficial) for the man to be alone;
I will make him a help, one who balances him—a counterpart
who is suitable and complementary for him."
~ Genesis 2:18 (AMP)

Before going any further, if you are a husband, I invite you to skip to the next chapter because the following is none of your business. The scriptures directed toward the wife are between your wife and God! However, if you are a saved, unmarried male seeking a wife, these are the attributes you should be looking for in your wife to be. When you do marry, the aforementioned rule would then apply. If you are a saved, single female, please don't write this off as not applicable to you because Isaiah 54:5 states you are already a wife, for your Maker is your Husband—the Lord Almighty is His Name. Apply to God what He requires for a wife and you'll be in total practice to honor a natural, God-centered Husband, if or when you are found by one (Proverbs 8:35).

The Wife

Our society's view of a wife's role when I was growing up encompassed a wide variety of archetypes: from subservient Edith Bunker to overbearing Rosanne, from stay-at-home Mom Carol Brady to family-oriented and career-minded Claire Huxtable as well as the negligent, narcissistic Peggy Bundy and every nuance in between! I can imagine we grieve God when we neglect His Word for the dissipation of mainstream's lack of understanding. In the Amplified version of Hosea 4:6, God proclaims, *"My people are destroyed for lack of knowledge of My law."* The Message Bible states that *"we are ruined because we do not know what is right or true."* The reason we do not know is because we neglect God's Word!

Ephesians 5:22 instructs wives to submit to their own husbands. Submit does not mean you are to lay down and allow him to walk on, step on, or kick you—literally or figuratively! The Greek word for submit is *hypotassō* (hü-po-tä's-sō), it is a verb and means to subject one's self, obey, to yield to one's admonition or advice. Sounds scary, I know. If you take submit all by itself and disregard the fullness of the scripture, yes it can seem categorically frightening to subject one's self to an emotionally driven and fundamentally flawed individual.

However, scripture does not tell wives to do that. God clarifies this command by adding *"as unto the Lord."* The Message Bible reads, *"Wives, understand and support your husbands in ways that show your support for Christ. The husband provides leadership to his wife the way Christ does to His church, not by domineering but by cherishing. So just as the church submits to Christ as He exercises such leadership, wives should likewise submit to their husbands"* (Ephesians 5:22-24). This doesn't mean a wife is to obey her husband as she would obey the Lord. This means she is to obey her husband as he is *yielded* to the Lord.

Look at 1 John 4:1, which warns us to carefully weigh and examine what we are told. Not everyone who talks about spiritual things is spiritual. The Spirit of God in a wife will bear witness to the Spirit of God in her husband because they are one and God is not the author of confusion! The Holy Spirit will speak to both for unity and clarity if they come together and submit unto Christ (1 Corinthians 12:11 MSG). If there is no lining up with the Word in a husband's words or actions on the matter at hand, the wife is not subject to that command. This is also why 2 Corinthians 6:14 admonishes, *"Do not be unequally yoked together with unbelievers. For what fellowship has righteousness with lawlessness? And what communion has light with darkness"* (NKJV)?

It is a dangerous thing for a Woman of God to deliberately place herself under the authority of an unsaved man or a saved one with ungodly ways or differing ideals. Yes, even if he is saved, you can still be unequally yoked! Ask yourself, how can two people walk together without agreeing on the direction (Amos 3:3)? Do not be deceived, different foundations in doctrinal theory can be a major issue. However, practical things from how to raise the children to how to spend the money can make a couple unequally yoked as well. It is the compilation of little things that spoil and ruin the vineyards of love (Solomon 2:15).

God has called us to allow peace to rule in our hearts and minds, not lust or desperation (Colossians 3:15, Romans 8:6). Marrying a man you know is not saved, who is carnal or does not honor God, lacks wisdom. Even wedding one who is opposed to your fundamental, provincial beliefs is an act of desperation and shows a lack of Faith in God's Promise to take care of everything you need. His generosity exceeds what you can even know to ask for or think, according to the Glory that comes from Christ Jesus (Philippians 4:19, Ephesians 3:20).

Now, if you, out of ignorance, desperation, or immorality, have married an unsaved man or did so when you also did not know the Lord, I have good news for you. All is not lost! You don't have to run down to the courthouse to throw him away so you can "believe God" for a saved man! Repent, ask God's forgiveness, and after you have sincerely repented, trust He has really forgiven you (1 John 1:9). Then, from here on out, rely on, be obedient to, and trust in God's Word! This is also your opportunity to be used by God like a Lighthouse on a hilltop—so shine!

Openly live like Christ before your husband. If he is not saved, he'll wonder and inquire about the change and may be persuaded toward Christ. If he is saved, you may prompt him to open up more with his own relationship with God (Matthew 5:16 MSG). Get stoked because you no longer have to lean to your own understanding, but acknowledge God in your marriage, shine forth His Will, and let His Faith lead you, in His Truth. Let go and allow the light of Christ to overtake the fabric of your marriage, so Love may abound. It all starts with you!

I wondered why Ephesians mentions the wife's role first and the husband's second. Since he's the Head and all, why not mention his role first? I believe I've figured it out. In the Amplified version of Proverbs 18:22, God encourages the man to find a wife, because by doing so he'll find a good life—and even more—favor and approval from God! If you are saved and yielded to God as *His* wife, you will be able to yield to your natural husband with no problem. God's Standards are higher than man's. If you are determined to increase in the wisdom and knowledge of God, you will please God. Whatever your responsibilities are as wife, do it from your soul, put in your very best effort, because you are really doing it unto the Lord and not your husband.

Know with all certainty that it is from the Lord, not your husband, that you will receive the inheritance, which is your greatest reward. It is the Lord Christ whom you actually serve in your marriage. If your husband is doing wrong, he will be dealt with for his wrongdoing. However, if you are in disobedience, God will also deal with you because there is no partiality or special treatment based on a person's position (Luke 2:52, Colossians 3:23-25).

This is another reason it is important to be equally yoked. Even though you are married to your husband, if he is saved, he is also your brother in Christ! When he acts up, you can go tell Daddy on him! Trust the Word! When the time has come for judgment, God will begin with His own household, so make sure when you go to Daddy on your brother, you have not thrown a rock and hidden your hands (1 Peter 4:17, 2 Corinthians 13:5). If he is not saved, he is of another family, so you will have to take authority over his father the devil, in order to see any real results. This is spiritual warfare, and you have Power over all the power of the enemy, use it (Luke 10:19)!

God started with the wife when He imparted the roles because, believe it or not, it is easier for you to be a wife than it is for your husband to be a husband. Why? Easy—as a saved woman, you are already a wife to God *and* you've had practice submitting. You were given practice every time you were obedient to what God's Word said. Every time you were tuned in to Him and flowed with His Spirit, you were being "wifely."

Even if you are newly saved, from a natural standpoint, think of how many times have you had to yield or concede because you were female? This is submission. Even if you have been submitting to the wrong things and in the wrong ways, you have been doing it your whole life. It is how God fearfully and wonderfully made you. Of course, He'd rather you submit to the right things as opposed to the wrong ones!

Your husband on the other hand, most likely has had zero, ninguno, nada—no time being a husband. If he has not spent time in the Word to find out how to be a Godly husband, or if he was not in the position to have had a God-fearing Father to teach him, he knows ZILTCH about how to be a husband to you. God only gave you two commands: to submit and to reverence. That's it. Your husband has a much longer list and a greater penalty if he doesn't comply! Also, what comes naturally to you, he has to actually work at!

It used to really bother me to hear a woman refer to her husband as if he were another one of her children. You know what I mean, if she had two children, she would refer to her husband as her third child. I hated that! I thought it to be so disrespectful, but now I understand it! It is a secular, fleshly way of saying a wife makes her husband better! It's not that she is his Mother to raise him, but is his *help* to better him! Help fit for him.

Since he generally comes into the marriage with no practical working knowledge or Godly experience at being a husband, God gave him you. Not as a blunt instrument to enforce change, but as a help to import destiny. As a woman of God you are already a wife. Already his help. NOT HIS HELPER! There is a difference.

Genesis 2:18 reads, "*And the Lord God said, it is not good that the man should be alone; I will make him an help meet for him.*" Help meet here, in Greek, is `ezer (ā›·zer), which means help or one who helps. Helper, according to Webster's Dictionary, means a person or thing that helps, gives assistance to or support. A synonym to helper is worker. A worker takes orders and gets with the program already in place or formerly established. A Help is not a help*er*—a mindless drone that follows orders. The Strongs Concordance is clear; the word help (`ezer) means just that—help.

Help has a plethora of connotations. It is limitless and vast. Psalm 46:1 assures us, *"God is our refuge and strength, a very present [Help] in trouble."* Help mentioned here is `ezrah, the *same* word derivative found in Genesis 2:18 and has the ***exact same*** definition. Does God do our bidding? Is He our mindless drone, do we order Him around? No! He empowers us, strengthens and directs us. He also confronts us, encourages and comforts us when we need Him most! This is what you are to your husband. You are help, fit and established by God for your husband, not help for how your husband sees fit! Think about it. If he does not know or realize that he needs help, how is he going to know to ask for it, or even know what to ask for?

There is an awe inspiring, spiritually uplifting painting by artist Kevin A. Williams aptly named *As One*, that I believe perfectly embodies God's Design for familial direction. I imagine as I gaze upon his beautiful illustration of a husband caring his wife and son on his back up a mountain: The Husband, obviously strong and capable, has his family firmly secured as he focuses on the upward goal. The Wife, fit and free from the burden of the climb, views and scans the trail ahead. She can see the loose rock to the left to inform him of the unstable toehold and warn him of the snake hiding in the crevice to the right in order to avoid. When she feels the lethargy in his chest and the fatigue in his legs, she can alert him to the oasis a few yards up to rest.

She is unstressed, having entrusted her husband to God. She listens to her husband's directions unchallenged, having the Word of God to weigh them by. She also has the freedom to be a strong and positive example as she teaches their child, firmly secured to her back about the climb, the path and their direction. With the child being a son, I can imagine she speaks highly of her husband as she tells the child how, when he's older, his Dad will show him how to climb. This is your God given power as a Wife. Your God given authority as a Mother.

A major part of honoring your husband is knowing your place in his life. You are his equal, a joint heir with him, part of his body, the protector of his heart (Galatians 3:28, Romans 8:17, Genesis 2:22, Mark 10:8). The scriptures never tell a wife to Love her husband.

The reason I believe this specific command is omitted is because it takes *God* (*Love*) for a woman to submit! If you are having trouble submitting to your husband, it is not his fault! This bears repeating: **If you are having trouble submitting to your husband, it is not his fault!**

Okay, if you happen to be married, the string of denials emanating from within your soul may mirror these: "But you don't know my husband!" or "He won't listen!" or "He always thinks he's right!" or "He won't take the lead!" or (fill in the blank!). It does not matter what he does or does not do! Submission is an act of Love based on trust, mutual consideration and Faith, not in your husband, but IN GOD! It's a Love issue and therefore a God Issue! You are to appreciate and support your husband in ways that show your support for Christ. It is not trust in your mate, but trust in God that supports your willingness to submit. Submission to your husband is submission to God's Word, not to man's understanding.

Yielding to your husband's way, if it does not line up with God's Way, is enabling (refer to Chapter Six). Enabling allows the enemy to reign through a lack of understanding the Power we have over him through Christ. Webster defines enabling as conferring new legal powers or capacities, having the right to license or regulate, giving authorization to. When you enable your husband (or anyone for that matter), you are giving him the right over your choices, power over your outcomes and authorization over your soul. This is never an option!

You should give no one that power but God. Romans 14:12 reminds us that each of us will give a personal account to God. If you have given your personal account over to your husband, do you think God will go to *him* for the detailed explanation at *your* life's conclusion? 2 Corinthians 5:10 clearly states, "*For we must all appear before the judgment seat of Christ; that everyone may receive the things done in his body, according to what he hath done, whether it be good or bad.*"

Cheerfully pleasing God is the main thing, and that's what your aim should be as wife, regardless of the conditions. Eventually you will have to face God concerning your activities. You will appear before Christ and face what's coming to you as a result of your actions and your choices, so make sure those actions and choices for which you will be judged are actually your own. You only lose yourself as a woman when you yield to other people's standards and disregard *God's* Purpose for your life.

Mark Twain said it best, "The two most important days in your life are the day you were born and the day when you find out why." Do not place yourself in the position to have to give another person's account because you have given authorization of your choices over to them.

In Ephesians 5:33b, God also commands that you respect or reverence your husband. Reverence here in Greek is *phobeō* (fo-be'-ō) and means to put to flight by terrifying, to be struck with fear or amazement. This is where the word phobia gets its root. *Phobeō* also means to venerate or worship (Yep! Now you see where Fabio got his name!), to treat with deference and reverential obedience. I thought it strange that the first two definitions dealt with fear and the last one dealt with honor. This is very significant.

I believe the first part of the definition "to put to flight by terrifying" is not directing you to fear your husband obviously, because God has not given you a spirit of fear. It is instead directing you to put to flight any evil, ungodly, disrespectful or destructive thought or deed, so you will be *able* to venerate and treat your husband with deference and reverential obedience. I believe God requires this because it will encourage you as you do so. It takes your eyes off your husband's actions, of which you have little overall control, and puts them on your own actions of which you do have some modicum of control (Philippians 4:13). Especially if your husband is saved and heading in the right direction, when you honor this God-centered choice, it will produce more after its kind. This is not possible if you are concentrating on your husband's faults and looking for more each day.

One thing is certain, when you look for something hard enough, you will eventually find it whether it is real or perceived. This being the case, look for and concentrate on the good things about your husband. You married him after all! Surely there is *something* you can pinpoint to be grateful for? Pick it and revel in it. This is Love! It empowers you as you fix your thoughts on what is true, and honorable, and right, and pure, and lovely, and admirable. Think about things that are excellent and worthy of praise (Philippians 4:8). As you do so, you'll increasingly discover more positive things to be thankful for!

It is important to understand the truth about submission as well as the need to reverence. These tools are God-given and God-inspired avenues of strength to commission and empower you as a woman first and then as a wife. Submission has calculably been given a very bad reputation in order to keep you weak through ignorance and deception and out of the Power that is yours through implementation of submission's quiet, yet potent Grace!

Submission is *not* blindly following where your husband leads. It is not an outward disposition, but an inner beauty of the hidden person of the heart, with the imperishable quality and unfading charm of a gentle and peaceful spirit, one that is calm and self-controlled, not overanxious, but serene and spiritually mature, which is very precious in the sight of God (1 Peter 3:4).

Submission is freedom to purposely follow God's Direction. Period! If your husband happens to be leading you in that direction, great! It's how God intended it to be. If your husband is not saved or saved and just stubborn, this does not absolve you of your God ordained directive found in Ephesians 5:22. Submission is still trusting God in the situation and not focusing on what your husband does, or is not doing in the environment in which you find yourself.

Also understand, reverencing your husband is not worshiping the ground on which he walks. It is instead choosing to remain awake and vigilant, not allowing the enemy to sow seeds of judgment, discontentment and antagonism in the soil of your soul toward your husband. The planting is allowed to occur by your consent alone (Matthew 13:25-29 AMP). Do not give your consent!

The Bible is clear and warns us not to be deceived because no one makes a fool of God. What you plant, you will harvest. If you ignore God's laid out injunctions to seed and fertilize your ground with compassion, acceptance and forgiveness, fueled by His all sufficient Grace, and choose to instead allow the plantings of mistrust, discontentment, and hostility by yourself or by others to take root in your soul, the full-grown harvest will strangle the emotional bond to your husband within your heart creating a pathway for the enemy to steal your resolve, kill your focus and destroy your marriage (Galatians 6:7; 2 Corinthians 9:8; John 10:10 AMP).

Plant seeds in response to God's Word, letting God's Spirit do the growth work in you. Be all the more diligent to make certain God's Call, His choosing you to be His wife, is not a grievous one. Remember you are God's wife first, so make sure that your behavior reflects and confirms your relationship with Him. By submitting to the Lordship of Christ in your husband (or following God's directions toward him as an unbeliever) and honoring his position as Head, you will actively develop the virtues of Christ to help you not stumble in your spiritual growth and will live an exemplary life (Isaiah 54:5; 2 Peter 1:10 AMP).

When you let go of your own understanding and are willing to suffer not getting your way or the injury of hurt feelings in respectful peace as God has entrusted you to do, not avenging yourself, it is then and only then, that you will see the Salvation of the Lord and His Victory in your home! God has tasked you with the betterment of your mate, but not the responsibility of his choices. Honor the position *of* Head and pray for the man *in* the position of authority, so that you can live a peaceful and quiet life marked by godliness and dignity (1 Timothy 2:1, 2 AMP).

God has entrusted you with this duty because He knows you have everything within you already to accomplish the task, as long as you rely upon Him to do it through you! God will never task you with something beyond your need for His Empowerment, so be strong in Him and take courage. Don't be intimidated. Don't give your husband a second thought. It is a wonderful thing if your husband is an honorable person even though he may get on your nerves from time to time. It makes it much more challenging however, if your husband is unsaved or saved and carnal. Either way, rest in the fact that God is calling you to honor the *position* of Headship that *He* has established not necessarily the person who holds it, especially if the person is dishonorable (Romans 13:1; Deuteronomy 31:6).

By honoring Headship, you honor God. This is why God tells you to take your eyes off your husband and put your eyes on Him. Also, be mindful of the fact that *you* made your husband your head. God did not say vows to him or sign the papers—you did. Now that you have, your obedience to what God's Word is telling you to do and your trust in His Intervention will move God, your God, to stride ahead of you and make your way sure. The rough places in your life will be made plain and the crooked places will be made straight. The Glory of the Lord shall be revealed through you and everyone will be able to see God's Hand upon your life (Isaiah 45:2, 40:4-5).

One very important thing to note here is what was discussed back in Chapter Six about accepting others' free will. If your unbelieving husband leaves you, you are free to let him go. Unbelieving here is *apistos* (ä›-pē-stos) in the Greek and means unfaithful, faithless, not to be trusted, perfidious—without trust in God. No matter what he is telling you on why he's leaving, even if he claims to be a Christian, it is his *actions* of breaking covenant that shows he is without trust in God, so you don't have to hold on desperately if he wants to go. God has released you and called you to make the best of it, as peacefully as you can (Romans 12:19; 1 Corinthians 7:15).

However, if you know you have been an unfaithful or shrewish wife to your husband (causing him to seek rooftop tranquility: Proverbs 21:9), repent and then begin to honor his position as God's Word instructs you to do. You never know, the way you handle this might cause your husband to change his mind, turn back to God or help him along the road toward Christ if he's not saved. Either way, trust God because He will be right there with you. He won't let you down. *He* won't leave you. He will repay wrong and He will reward obedience (Proverbs 25:24; 2 Peter 1:10; Deuteronomy 31:6; Psalm 19:11)!

It is true that whatever issues you face won't go away overnight, but trust God and have Faith that He will help you if you yield to *His* Wisdom. Take your marriage (if you are single, take your everyday life: your sleeping, eating, going-to-work, and walking-around life) and place it before God as an offering. Embracing what God has promised you is the best thing you can do to honor

Him as well as yourself. Don't become so well-adjusted to what the world has told you marriage is or what your life's direction should be as a single woman, that you fit into it without even thinking and disregard what God commands (Romans 12:1, 2, 19 MSG).

Instead, live your life on purpose and fix your attention on Him. You'll be changed from the inside out. Readily recognize what He wants from you as a Wife (you are His wife as well after all), and quickly respond to it. This is Faith's framework for being Fit Help! Unlike the culture around you, always dragging you down to its level of immaturity and ungodliness, God will bring the best out of you and develop a well-formed maturity in you, so be fearless (Philippians 2:13; Deuteronomy 11:26-28; 2 Timothy 1:7 AMP)!

Chapter Twelve

HEADSHIP OF CHRIST

For this reason a man shall leave his father and his mother, and shall be joined to his wife; and they shall become one flesh.
~ Genesis 2:24 (AMP)

Before going any further, as with the last chapter, if you are a wife, I invite you to skip to the next chapter because the following is none of your business. The scriptures directed toward the husband are between your husband and God. However, if you are a saved, unmarried female seeking to be found by a Man of God, these are the attributes you should be looking for in the man you will place in the position of Headship over your life. When you do marry, the aforementioned rule would then apply. If you are a saved, single man please pay close attention before you rush into seeking and finding a wife. It is important to learn all you can about what God requires on how to Love her. The Bible promises blessings to the man who finds his wife. However, the flipside is the tremendous cost to you when you mistreat one of God's precious daughters (Malachi 2:13-15 MSG).

The Husband

Our society's view of a husband's role runs the gambit: from stalwart Ward Cleaver and hilarious Michael Kyle to narrow-minded Archie Bunker and hard-working yet humble Carl Winslow; from dimwitted Homer Simpson to violently deranged Walter White and all the *Shades of Grey* between them! I can imagine we grieve God when the lurid portrayals of Husbands and Fathers in the media are mirrored in real life scenarios among professing Christian men. When His Word is neglected for the drivel of mainstream's lack of understanding, and slanted views of masculinity result, is it no wonder the family lies broken and battered—trampled under the feet of this reckless behavior? This irresponsible, careless conduct has consequently imprisoned families into an unrestrained, indecorously blasphemous circumstance!

In the Amplified version of Hosea 4:6, God proclaims, *"My people are destroyed for lack of knowledge of My law."* The Message Bible states that *"we are ruined because we do not know what is right or true."* The reigns of the runaway carriage of life must be taken in hand. The only one capable, called, authorized, and ordained by God to do this is you! Yes, you! As Sean Connery says in Columbia Pictures' American drama film, *Finding Forester*, "You're the man now, Dawg!"

The Spirit of God in a wife will bear witness to the Spirit of God in her husband because they are one and God is not the Author of confusion. The Holy Spirit can Speak to both for unity and clarity (1 Corinthians 12:11 AMP). If you want your wife to listen to you, then you as her husband need to listen to God. Your Headship (which is by God's Ordained Design) must line up with God's Word in how you verbally express yourself, as well as in your actions, in order for your wife to even be *able* to hear you when you speak to her.

God is so offended with the disregard of His Word and the lack of understanding toward her that He refuses to even listen when *you* speak to Him! It is a trickle-down effect. God won't hear you, so neither can she. You must realize that the Bible is emphatic about this: she is your equal, a joint heir with you and a part of your own body (1 Peter 3:7 AMP, Galatians 3:28, Romans 8:17, Mark 10:8, Genesis 2:22).

The Bible also warns, while the lips of an immoral woman are as sweet as honey, and her mouth is smoother than oil, in the end she is as bitter as poison, as dangerous as a double-edged sword. Her feet go down to death; her steps lead straight to the grave for she cares nothing about the path to life. She staggers down a crooked trail and doesn't even realize it (Proverbs 5:3-8).

This is why 2 Corinthians 6:14 admonishes, *"Do not be unequally yoked together with unbelievers. For what fellowship has righteousness with lawlessness? And what communion has light with darkness"* (NKJV)? Her outer package may *rock,* but her inner one, the one that counts, may make your brain *roll* inside your skull! The Bible warns she will drive you to climb up on the rooftop of your own house in an effort to get away from her, just to get some peace (Proverbs 21:9)!

Another reason to be equally yoked is the fact that even though you are married to your wife, if she is saved, she is also your sister in Christ! When she acts up, you can go tell Papa on her! Trust the Word! When the time has come for judgment, God will begin with His own household, so make sure when you go to Papa on your sister, you have not thrown a rock and hidden your hands! If she is not saved, she is of another family, so you will have to take authority over her father the devil, in order to see any real results. This is spiritual warfare and you have Power over all the power of the enemy—use it (1 Peter 4:17, 2 Corinthians 13:5; Luke 10:19)!

It is a dangerous thing for a Godly Man to deliberately cleave unto an unsaved woman, a saved one with ungodly ways or one with differing ideals. Yes, even if she is saved, you can still be unequally yoked! Ask yourself, how two people can walk together without agreeing on the direction (Amos 3:3)? Having different foundations in doctrinal theory is a major issue however, practical things like how to raise the children to how often to have sex can make you unequally yoked. It is the compilation of little things that spoil and ruin the vineyards of Love. God has called us to allow peace to rule in our hearts and minds, not lust or desperation (Solomon 2:15; Colossians 3:15, Romans 8:6).

Marrying a woman you know is not saved, carnal or opposed to your fundamental, provincial beliefs is an act of desperation and shows a lack of Faith in God's Promise to take care of everything you need. His generosity exceeds what you can even know to ask for or think, according to the Glory that's imparted through Christ Jesus. Now if you, out of ignorance, desperation or immorality, have married an unsaved woman or did so when you did not know the Lord, I have good news for you! All is not lost! Repent, ask God's forgiveness and when you have sincerely repented, trust He has actually forgiven you (Philippians 4:19, Ephesians 3:20; 1 John 1:9).

Then, from here on out, rely on, be obedient to and trust in God's Word! You'll be off that rooftop before you know it! This is your opportunity to be used by God like a Lighthouse on a hilltop— so shine! Openly live like Christ before your wife. If she is not saved, she'll wonder and inquire about the change and may be persuaded toward Christ. If she is saved, you may prompt her to open up more with her relationship with God (Matthew 5:16 MSG).

It's time to get stoked because you no longer have to lean to your own understanding, but acknowledge God in your marriage and shine forth His Will and let His Faith lead you, in His Truth! Allow the light of Christ to overtake the fabric of your marriage, so Love may abound. If you are a saved single man, allow the light of Christ to overtake the fabric of your life in such a way that if or when you find your wife, the knowledge of how you should treat her will be instinctual. God will be able to literally Love her through you! It all starts with you!

If you are having trouble Loving your wife, it is not her fault! This statement bears repeating: **If you are having trouble Loving your wife, it is not her fault!** Okay, if you happen to be married, the string of denials emanating from within your soul may mirror these "But you don't know my wife!" or "She won't listen!" or "She always thinks she is right!" or "She can be a first class (you know)!" or (fill in the blank!).

What she does or does not do. How she acts or does not act! Does not matter! Choosing to Love her is based on trust, mutual consideration and Faith, not in your wife, but IN GOD! It's a Love issue and therefore a God issue! You are to Love and cherish your wife in ways that show you Love and cherish Christ. Again, it is not trust in your mate, but trust in God that supports your willingness to Love her. Ephesians 5: 25-33 instructs:

> *Husbands, Love your wives, even as Christ also loved the church, and gave himself for it; That He might sanctify and cleanse it with the washing of water by the word, that he might*

101

present it to himself a glorious church, not having spot, or wrinkle, or any such thing; but that it should be holy and without blemish. So ought men to love their wives as their own bodies. He that loveth his wife loveth himself. For no man ever yet hated his own flesh; but nourisheth and cherisheth it, even as the Lord the church: For we are members of his body, of his flesh, and of his bones. For this cause shall a man leave his father and mother, and shall be joined unto his wife, and they two shall be one flesh. This is a great mystery: but I speak concerning Christ and the church. Nevertheless let every one of you in particular so love his wife even as himself.

Wow, that is a great deal to take in! It may seem too daunting a task, so we shall take each step, one by one. The scriptures state that you are to *Love* your wife as Christ *Loves* the Church. Love here is *agapaō* (ä-gä-pä›-ō) in Greek and means to welcome, entertain, be fond of, well pleased and contented with. This was mentioned in a previous chapter and bears repeating; *agapaō*, is a derivative of *agapē* (God's Love) not *philia* (brotherly), *storge* (familial) or even *eros* (romantic).

This is very significant in translation. This designates God's very Presence in His Command to you, to Love your wife. *He will do it through you* as you *yield* to Him and not to your own understanding on how this is done. In all your ways know and acknowledge, recognize, trust, and yield to Him, and He will make your paths straight and smooth. He'll remove obstacles that block your way or strengthen you to stand when you have been obedient to His Word concerning His Standard of Love (Hebrews 13:20-21, Proverbs 3:5-6, Ephesians 6:13).

First, understand that the Love you are to have for your wife is *selfless*. Remember, less is more (refer to Chapter One). Love is self*LESS*! Since she is part of your "own body," this Love toward her is marked by giving, not getting. Just as you give to yourself without reservation, you are to give unto her with the same intensity and forbearance.

Second, this Love sanctifies her. Sanctify here is *hagiazō* (hä-gē-ä'-zō) in Greek and means to purify by expiation: free from the guilt of sin by a renewing of the soul. You cannot save her soul, but you can help renew it. You are tasked with making her a better woman by aiding in *healing* her emotional and mental hurts, not in *causing* them. Overbearing, domineering tactics only crush your wife's spirit, making her withdraw into herself, or it will bring out the Zena Warrior Princess in her and then you'll have a real fight on your hands!

Ephesians 5: 23-24 in The Message Bible reads, "*The husband provides leadership to his wife the way Christ does to His church, not by domineering but by cherishing. So just as the church submits to Christ as He exercises such leadership, wives should likewise submit to their husbands.*" This means submission is not one sided!

In God's Chain of Command, your wife's submission is predicated upon your submission to God's Directive to lead according to Christ's Example toward His Church. If you are hard, harsh and, pressing, or lethargic and uninterested, you disqualify yourself of this God Empowered Submission. Conversely, when you cherish her, you help her mature into the woman of God she is meant to be—God Authored Submission then follows. As she increases in her Life hid with Christ in God, the better wife she will be to you! Better wife means better friend, and better friend means better lover. *Think about that!*

Cherish here is *thalpō* (thä'l-pō) in Greek and means to foster with tender care. According to Webster, foster means to promote the growth or development of. Christ's Love makes the Church whole, and His Words evoke her beauty. Everything Christ does and says is designed to bring the best out of her, dressing her in dazzling white silk, radiant with holiness. This is your example! This is how you are to Love your wife. You'll really be doing yourself a favor since you are already "one" with her in marriage. You would not think to abuse or hurt your own body on purpose, would you? No, you feed and pamper yourself, not withholding any good thing from yourself. This is how Christ treats the Church, because she is part of His Body (Ephesians 5:28, 29, Psalm 84:11).

The third way you are to Love your wife is to remember, you are commanded in Ephesians 5:31 to leave your father and your mother and are to prize your wife above your parents and all others.

Leave here is *kataleipō* (kä-tä-lā'-pō) and means to forsake, leave to one's self a person or thing by ceasing to care for it, to abandon it. This is a mental and emotional shifting of loyalties.

Your Wife comes before Mom and Dad, as well as siblings in allegiance, because she is now part of you. Your wife is the only person you can be one with. Parents, children, and best friends don't count. It is not only a physical oneness if you both are saved, but a Spiritual one as well, designed and empowered by God through Christ. You are no longer two, but have become "one flesh." The Apostle Paul calls it a huge mystery, but makes it clear that Jesus' example of how He treats the Church provides a good picture of how you are to treat your wife. You are in effect Loving yourself when you Love your wife (1 Corinthians 6:17; Ephesians 5:25-33). This is the Love Christ has for His Bride—The Church!

Another major part of Loving your wife is not only knowing your place in her life but also knowing her role in yours. Contrary to popular belief, YOUR WIFE IS NOT YOUR HELPER, she is instead Help *fit* for you. There is a difference. Genesis 2:18 reads, *"And the Lord God said, it is not good that the man should be alone; I will make him an help meet for him."* Help meet here in Greek is `*ezer* (ā>-zer) and means help or one who helps. Helper, according to Webster, means person or thing that helps, but goes on to say gives assistance to, support. A synonym to helper is worker. A worker takes orders and gets with the program already in place or formerly established. A Help is not a help*er*—a mindless drone that follows orders.

The Strongs Concordance is clear; the term help meet (`*ezer*) means just that—help. Help has a plethora of connotations. It is limitless and vast. Psalm 46:1 assures us, *"God is our refuge and strength, a very present [Help] in trouble."* Help mentioned here is `*ezrah*, the same word derivative found in Genesis 2:18 and has the **exact same** definition. Does God do our bidding? Is He our mindless drone, do we order Him around? No! He empowers us, strengthens and directs us. He also confronts us, encourages and comforts us when we need Him most!

Your wife is help for you, fit, and established by God. She has been given as help for you as your wife, not help for how you see fit as her husband. Think about it. If you do not have a clue in a situation, wouldn't it be nice to have a free-thinking agent at your disposal who can *also* hear from God instead of a mindless drone awaiting orders? This is God's earthly backing for you! He made you Head with Help! Much of life's pressure is freed when its burden is shared.

There is an awe inspiring, spiritually uplifting painting by artist Kevin A. Williams aptly named *As One*, that I believe perfectly embodies God's Design for familial direction. I imagine as I gaze upon his beautiful illustration of a husband, caring his wife and son on his back up a mountain: The Husband, obviously fit, strong and capable, has his wife and son firmly secured to his back. I can imagine he has imparted expectations to his wife and now has given her over to God, trusting Him to inspire her to do what is necessary for him and their child, as he focuses on *his* goal, the upward climb. It is intuitive that he does not have her at his front, cradled in His arms as if she is helpless or so he can keep an eye on her every move, as this would distract him from his purpose as well as hinder his ability to use his arms for the climb or to defend his family if necessary.

Another reason it is wise of him not to have her at his front, facing him in a second position, wrapped around his middle, is because this would place his wife's back toward the mountain to conceivably cause her damage against its rough and jagged face. Also, with the mountain at her back, she would be forced to cradle their son to her front; causing the child to be in an untenable position, to possibly get crushed between his parents during some of the more arduous aspects of their upward momentum.

They would also counterbalance the man in a frontward position, as well as hinder his ability to move and grab for sure grips up the mountain's side. With his family firmly secured to his back, his hands can be easily unrestricted to defend and protect his family. He is also free from distraction to note the sun's (a metaphor for Jesus) position in the sky in order tell the time of day as well as their location (another metaphor for God's Will), to be assured of his direction. He's free to perceive the conditions of the atmosphere, to note the advent of seasonal changes and coming storms in order to relay and confer with his wife and to reassure and instruct his son.

If a storm does come, no matter how loud the thunder or how strong the winds, his wife's voice is right by his ear with necessary aid, without him having to take his eyes off the goal because he has her perfectly positioned, as well as his son for instruction. This is your God given responsibility as a husband. Your God given authority as a Father.

The choice to Love your wife purposefully, actively, and with a sincere heart, is based not on secular understanding, but on a willingness to believe and trust in God's Word. Allowing your wife to rule you is not of God just as vicious overbalance is also not of God. When you do not stand up in your Authority as a husband, you are not leading your house in the Way God has Ordained it to go. There is a difference between heeding the wise counsel of your wife and allowing her to run roughshod over you and your children. This is not how you Love her or your children.

Listening to your wife when the advice is not in line with God's Way or lying down on the job, so to speak, is enabling (refer to Chapter Six). Enabling allows the enemy to reign through a lack of understanding the Power we have over him through Christ. Webster defines enabling as conferring new legal powers or capacities, having the right to license or regulate, giving authorization to. When you enable your wife (or anyone for that matter) you are giving her the right over your choices, the outcome of your family, as well as the authorization over your very soul. This should never be an option!

You should give no one that power but God. Romans 14:12 reminds us that each of us will give a personal account to God. If you have given your personal account over to your wife, do you think God will go to *her* for the detailed explanation at *your* life's conclusion or that of the family to which *you* and you *alone* are Head? 2 Corinthians 5:10 clearly states, *"For we must all appear before the judgment seat of Christ; that everyone may receive the things done in his body, according to that he hath done, whether it be good or bad."*

The Bible states that if you and your wife are saved, you are joint *heirs* with Christ, not joint *Heads* of your house (Romans 8:17). Cheerfully pleasing God is the main thing, and that's what your aim should be as Husband, regardless of the conditions. Eventually, you will appear before Christ and face what's coming to you as a result of your actions or lack thereof, as well as the direction in which your family went. You are the Family's Head after all, so make sure the choices made are actually your own, filtered through and governed by the Light of God's Word and not those spawned from selfish desires, fears of not being able to control every aspect of the situation, or any other fears inspired by the enemy.

Mark Twain said it best, "The two most important days in your life are the day you were born and the day when you find out why." Do not place yourself in the position to have to give another person's account because you have given authorization of your choices over to them. Allowing yourself to be puppeteered, or being on autopilot throughout your life, is never an option for a Man of God! You only get caught up in the vicissitudes of life when you yield to other ideals and disregard God's Standard and Purpose for your life. The Ashley Madison websites of the world and gallivanting off to Vegas—let me just pause here to say that "whatever happens in Vegas" can put you into an early grave, so don't fall for that misnomer no matter how catchy it sounds!

Anyway, the Ashley Madison style websites, gallivanting off to Vegas, pharmaceutical binges, or whatever—no matter what the proverbial *"they"* are trying to sell you—will have no actual appeal to you when you find and follow God's Purpose for your life. Purpose fixes focus! When you can fix your focus on what God has Purposed for you—in this case Loving your wife, or just Loving God if you are single—*HE* will empower you for what matters as a husband and father or what He has for you as a single Man of God. The beauty of it all is, His Purpose is what will bring you joy and fulfillment anyway! He made you, so He Knows you better than you know yourself (Jeremiah 17:10 NLT, Romans 8:27 MSG).

If you are married or single and want to get married, it is imperative to understand that having a wife, children, coveted career, or any outer pursuit will NOT give you what you need without

God being the Central Focus of everything you do. So your focus cannot be primarily on these things. God requires you to Love others as you Love yourself, especially in regard to Loving your wife because it takes your eyes off your wife's actions, of which you have no overall control, and puts them on your own of which you do have a modicum of control (Philippians 4:13). Especially if your wife is saved and heading in the right direction. When you respect and make God-centered choices, they will produce more after their kind.

Loving your wife will be a challenge if you are concentrating on her faults and looking for more each day. One thing is certain, when you look for something hard enough, you will find it— whether it is real or imagined. This being the case, look for and concentrate on the good things about your wife. You married her after all; surely there is *something* you can pinpoint to be grateful for? Pick it and revel in it. This is Love! It empowers you as you fix your thoughts on what is true, and honorable, and right, and pure, and lovely, and admirable. Think about things that are excellent and worthy of praise (Philippians 4:8). As you do this, you'll discover even more things to be grateful for in your wife and in your marriage!

It is imperative you understand the truth about the command to Love, as well as the need to take your Headship seriously and not passively. These directives are God-given and God-inspired avenues of strength to direct and empower you as a man. Being a Loving and especially an attentive husband, has been given a very bad reputation by the enemy in order to keep you weak through ignorance and deception and out of the Authority that is yours through the application of Love's ever increasing Power! Loving your wife does not make you weak. On the contrary, it is an avenue deliberately designed by God for you to have a good life and to bask in His Favor (Proverbs 18:22). It is freedom to intentionally follow God's Direction as He has carefully, strategically and tenaciously laid it out for you. Period!

God has taken all the guesswork out! Even where your wife is concerned. Proverbs 5:18 states, *"Let thy fountain be blessed: and rejoice with the wife of thy youth."* The Message Bible translation states: *"Enjoy the wife you married as a young man! Lovely as an angel, beautiful as a rose—don't ever quit taking delight in her body. Never take her Love for granted!"* Leave her to Him and work *with* Him on yourself as you plant the seed of God's Word in your wife's heart and in your Family's lives, through your everyday words. Water those words with your God-inspired actions and He'll do the rest (Deuteronomy 31:6; 1 Corinthians 3:6)!

If your wife is not saved or is saved, but hurt by your previous ill treatment of her due to your ignorance or misunderstanding of God's Word, or if she is just stubborn, following God's Command to Love is still trusting Him in the situation and not focusing on what your wife does, or is not doing in the environment in which you have allowed to transpire as Head.

Change the environment through the example of obedience. You are the one with the Authority to do so. Live with your wife in an understanding way and take conscious, deliberate delight in her. Use great gentleness and thoughtfulness with an intelligent regard for the marriage relationship you are sharing with her. Even if she seems as though she can handle things all on her own, deliberately show her honor and respect as your wife and as a fellow heir of the Grace of Life. When you do this, your relationship with her and with God will grow exponentially because your prayers will not be hindered or be ineffective (1 Peter 3:7 NLT).

Also understand, Loving your wife is choosing to remain awake and vigilant, not allowing the enemy to sow seeds of judgment, discontentment and antipathy in the soil of your soul toward your wife. It is by your consent this planting is allowed to occur. The Bible is clear and warns us not to be deceived because no one makes a fool of God. What you plant, you will harvest (Matthew 13:25; Galatians 6:7)

If you ignore God's laid out injunctions to seed and fertilize your ground with understanding, compassion, acceptance, and forgiveness, fueled by His all sufficient Grace, and choose to instead allow the plantings of mistrust, discontentment, jealousy, and hostility by yourself or by others, to take root in your soul, the full-grown harvest will strangle the emotional bond to your wife within your heart. This will create a pathway for the enemy to steal your focus, kill your resolve, and destroy your marriage. Plant seeds in response to God's Word and *allow* God's Spirit do the growth work in you (Galatians 6:8,9; John 10:10 AMP).

A very important thing to note here is what was discussed back in Chapter Six about accepting other's free will. If your unbelieving wife walks out, you do not have to chase her if she truly wants to leave. Unbelieving here is *apistos* (ä›-pē-stos) in the Greek and means unfaithful, faithless, not to be trusted, perfidious, without trust in God. No matter what she is telling you on why she's leaving, even if she claims to be a Christian, it is her *actions* of breaking covenant that shows she is without trust in God, so you don't have to hold on desperately if she wants to go. God has released you and called you to make the best of it, as peacefully as you can. However, if you know you have not been a faithful or Loving husband to your wife, repent and then begin to Love her as Christ Loves the Church (2 Peter 1:10; 1 Corinthians 7:15; Ephesians 5:25)!

A Kendrick Brother's film entitled *Fireproof*, is an excellent illustration of what can happen when a man gives his heart to God in true repentance. You never know, the way you handle this might cause your wife to change her mind, turn back to God or help her along the road toward Christ if she's not saved. Either way, trust God because He will be right there with you. He won't let you down. *He* won't leave you. *He* will repay wrong and *He* will reward obedience (1 Peter 5:7; Psalm 55:22; Hebrews 4:16; Psalm 19:11-13 MSG; Romans 12:19)!

It is true, the issues facing you won't go away overnight, but trust God and have Faith that He will help you as you yield to His Wisdom. Take your marriage (if you are single, take your everyday life—your sleeping, eating, going-to-work, and walking-around life) and place it before God as an offering. Embracing what God has promised you is the best thing you can do for yourself, as well as to honor Him (Romans 12:1, 2 MSG).

Don't become so well-adjusted to what the world has told you marriage is or what your life's direction should be as a single man, that you fit into it without even thinking and disregard God's dictates. Instead, fix your attention on Him. You'll be changed from the inside out. Readily recognize what He wants from you as a husband, as Head of your Family, or as a single Man of God. Unlike the culture around you, always dragging you down to its level of immaturity and ungodliness, God will bring the best out of you, so make sure that your behavior reflects and confirms your relationship with Him (John 10:10; Galatians 6:7).

This is Faith's framework for being the Headship of Christ! The Band Sanctus Real, capsulizes this God driven desire in their song *Lead Me*. By choosing to obey God's Command to Love your wife, you honor your own position as Head. This obedience will aggressively activate the virtues of Christ within you to help you not stumble in your Spiritual growth and will empower you to live a life that is an example to your wife, your children, and others as you exemplify the characteristics of a Man reflecting God's own Heart (2 Peter 1:10; Matthew 5:16)!

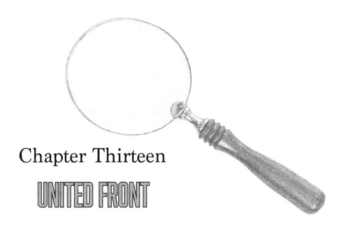

Chapter Thirteen

UNITED FRONT

"Marriage is more than four bare legs in a bed."
~ Hoshang N. Akhtar

There are many opinions out there on how to raise stable, responsible children who are viably fruitful and contribute favorably to our society. The only opinion that matters, however, is found in the Word of God. God's Opinion is the most important. He invented the whole process, so that makes Him the Ultimate Authority on the matter! Loving your child should be the interwoven thread throughout every dealing with your child. From conception to launching them out into the world, and beyond (because you never cease being a parent), the Bible is clear on how this process is to be accomplished. For the sake of limiting this to one chapter, we'll delve into what I believe are the four most important points, in order of importance.

The first step to being a great parent (being a great parent should be synonymous with Loving your child) is to show Love for one another as their parents. Marriage is the building block of any civilized society. It was the second human relationship God established in the Biblical Record—God's relationship with humankind being the first. Marriage creates family, family builds character, and character preserves relationships as ordained by God's established order (Genesis 2:21-25, 2:15). John 10:10a reads, *"The thief cometh not, but for to steal, and to kill, and to destroy."* This is a pivotal scripture because it is the motive behind why being a parent in today's world is one of the most important, as well as challenging occupations to date!

It is burdened with substantial oppositions in order to encourage dissention on every level of human development. If your marriage can be destroyed, or marriage in general done away with altogether, raising children in a secure, stable and God exalted environment is much more difficult and most impractical. The overwhelming spread of evil (sex without the benefit of marriage, adultery, deviant yet increasingly excepted sexual practices as well as the extension of gender designation beyond male and female) will do a society in. Nothing will be left of the people's Love but a mound of ashes (Matthew 24:12 MSG). Even though these sins have unfortunately led to situations in which every parent is not married to their child's other parent, showing Love one to another still applies. Love is not sexual. Love is a conscious choice, one to be civil, supportive, and productive.

If you are not married to your children's other biological parent, you are charged to pursue peace with that other individual for your children's sake if at all possible and not to retaliate against them. You've got it in you to get along with the other if you give it to God. Do not insist on getting even! Vengeance is not yours to dispense! God says He'll do the judging and then take care of the matter on the side of Truth if you rely upon Him and not yourself (Romans 12:18, 14:19; Mark 9:50; 1 Peter 3:11; Romans 8:28).

God's Original Design centered on whole family structures and was not intended as a competition nor as a partnership, but as a spiritually empowered, interworking, perpetual mechanism formulated to connect two lives through the communication of exchanging Biblical Truths in an effort to present God's Trinity based system here on earth.

In Mark 10: 5-9 Jesus confronts the Pharisees, a prevailing religious order of His day, concerning marriage and divorce. He told them that Moses wrote the precept of divorce only as a concession due to the hardhearted ways of the people. Jesus went on to state in the original creation, God made male and female to be together and because of this, a man leaves father and mother, and in marriage he becomes one flesh with his wife. They are no longer two individuals, but form a new entity and because God creates this organic union of the two opposite sexes, no one should desecrate His created sculpture by cutting them apart (MSG).

Sounds like God intended the union between a Husband and a Wife to be a permanent one. Just think about that. God sees a husband and wife as no longer two, but one flesh. Just as you are one with your arm, leg and other body parts. So, imagine you slept on your arm wrong so that when you woke up it was bothering you. I mean it's really aching something fierce! Would you just cut if off?! I don't think you would. Even, God forbid, if you were in a situation where cutting off a limb was actually a viable option, I still believe you'd seek any means necessary to stall or rectify the problem without amputation.

This is how marriage should be viewed; rectification of the problem so severing is not an option. It is also absolutely clear that God has called you to a free life which became yours by accepting all Jesus did for you through His death, burial, and resurrection. Just make sure that you don't use this freedom as an excuse to do whatever you want to do and destroy your freedom or your marriage (John 8:36; 1 Corinthians 15:1-4; Galatians 5:13).

Rather, use your freedom to serve one another in Love—it's how freedom grows. It is also how your marriage will grow. For everything we know about God's Word is summed up in a single sentence: Love others as God Loves you. This should most definitely, and with all due diligence, be applied to the one with whom you are actually one with! To do so is an act of true freedom (Galatians 5:13b; 1 Peter 2:16; John 15:12).

If you viciously devastate, damage and destroy each other, watch out! In no time at all, you will be annihilating one another, and where will your precious freedom or your marriage be then (Galatians 5:13-15)? As a child of God, you must understand and act as if you know His Spirit dwells within you. With Him being in you, He is therefore a part of your marriage whether you acknowledge this fact or not. It is to your advantage not only to acknowledge Him, but to *encourage* His cooperation!

When you face challenges and discouragements designed to overpower you or your mate, God intended for your mate to support you and for you to support your mate. When these challenges overpower you both, God is there to strengthen and encourage you both through His Word and by His Spirit. In this way He, your spouse and you are like a triple-braided cord, one not easily broken (Ecclesiastes 4:12).

The problem comes in when only one or neither parties are saved in the marriage, neither of the parties are married to one another, but are "playing house" or both are saved but have not allowed the Word of God to penetrate their hearts in order to effectively mold their lives. Having a personal relationship with God through His Son Jesus Christ and immersion in His Word for soul salvation is necessary for continued cohesiveness and productivity to prevail throughout a long and lasting union.

Marriage is an established, God Ordained Union and therefore should be approached as such. Not doing so is like opening a complex, unfamiliar product for the first time and expecting to be a pro at it without first reading the directions! Sure, you'll muddle through on your own, but how much damage, to the product as well as yourself, would be avoided had you just taken time to get proper guidance and instruction first!

You may be asking, "What does this have to do with raising kids?" Well…EVERYTHING! Loving God, the Source of Love, is the most important thing to the Life He's given you. You need His Ability to be *able* to Love your spouse effectively as well as sustainably! John 13:35 in the Amplified states, *"By this everyone will know that you are My disciples, if you have [Love]and unselfish concern for one another."* In this scripture, Jesus was speaking to His Disciples, directing their behavior toward one another as examples to unbelievers. As parents, you are dealing with unbelievers in your children. You didn't come out of your Mother's womb with the knowledge of God or Faith to believe and neither did nor will your child.

Just as The Romans Road to Salvation is an unpretentious, yet powerful way of explaining the Good News of Jesus Christ—how God provided Salvation through His Son, why we need Salvation, how we can receive Salvation, and what benefits Salvation provide—your life should be the Roman Road to Salvation for your child through application in daily living. You must be a United

Front in Loving one another, but primarily, your Love for God should shine through in this application more than anything else.

The second way to Love your children concerns praying and speaking God's Word over their lives before conception, after conception and every day after their birth. Prayer is essential in ongoing warfare, so pray diligently and unceasingly for your children. Pray individually and collectively, keeping your spiritual eyes open, staying alert and persistent in your prayers concerning your child's life's course (Ephesians 6:18,19 AMP; 1 Thessalonians 5:17; Deuteronomy 32:30).

According to Psalm 119:105 in The Amplified Bible, the Word of God is a lamp unto our feet that casts a beam of light on the dark paths of life, so it is important to focus that light daily through prayer and by speaking the Word of God over your children's lives. While prayer is essential, it must be backed with action. Proverbs 22:6 tells you to direct your children onto the right path, and when they are older, they will not leave it. That right path is navigated within God's Word.

King James Version reads, *"Train up a child in the way he should go and when he is old, he will not depart from it."* Unfortunately, many parents fail to train in the way the child *should* go, but inadvertently train in the way the child should *not* go, by virtue of what they focus on with their words. For instance, instead of harping on what you don't want by saying, "Stop fighting with your brother!" focus on what you do want by saying, "Treat your brother like you want to be treated."

Treating others as you want to be treated is based on Matthew 7:12 in the Amplified which reads, *"So then, in everything treat others the same way you want them to treat you, for this is the essence of the Law and the writings of the Prophets."* It may seem a simple concept, but it is an effective one. The Word does not lie and according to Romans 4:17, God gives life to the dead and can call into being what does not exist.

The King James reads, *"God, [Who] quickeneth the dead, and calleth those things which be not as though they were."* It does not read: calls those things that *are* as though they *are not*! Going back to the example, by calling out what is, "fighting" you are speaking what you don't want and telling it to stop, giving it credence and therefore more power. By instead calling out or focusing on the behavior you *do* want you are giving *it* Power and making *it* the focus.

Negativity is prolonged by focusing on it, just as positivity is perpetuated by focusing on it. Words can kill, or words can give life. They can be either poison or they can be fruit. You choose each day the ones you use to train and guide your children (Proverbs 18:21). Do not nullify your prayers *for* your children with the words you speak *over* your children. So, speak God's Word over their lives and you won't go wrong.

The third way to Love your children is to discipline them and not to punish them. A familiar scripture which has become the default position for many believers when it comes to disciplining their children, has been taken way out of context and unfortunately, to the extreme in some cases. Proverbs 22:15 states, *"Foolishness is bound in the heart of a child; but the rod of correction shall drive it far from him."* Rod in Hebrew is *shebet* (shā'·vet) and the first three meanings translate into staff, branch or club. The fourth meaning, and one I've not heard mentioned as readily as the first three, is *truncheon* or *scepter* and means mark of authority. What is our mark of authority as believers? The Word of God!

John 1:1 in the Amplified Bible is clear, *"In the beginning, before all time, was the Word (Christ), and the Word was with God, and the Word was God Himself."* Jesus being the Christ, the Son of the living God said, *"All Authority, all Power of Absolute Rule in heaven and on earth has been given to Me"* (AMP). *He* Is our Mark of Authority because we have this Authority and Power *through* Him! This makes us ambassadors for Christ, as though God were making His appeal through us (Matthew 28:18 AMP; 2 Corinthians 5:20).

Let's revisit Proverbs 22:15 with this in mind; it would then read something like this: "Foolishness is bound in the heart of a child; but the Word of God shall drive it far from him." It's a simple statement, but a Powerful Truth!

Our Mark of Authority (God's Word) is all Powerful! However, the rod of correction gets the attention focused in such a direct and uncompromising way. It's application is appropriate for the Word to penetrate the natural defenses that block the impartation of common sense. So don't be afraid to use corporal punishment to correct your children. Spanking, while not politically correct won't kill them. A good spanking, in fact, might save them from something worse—a reckless, narcissistic and obstreperous life (Proverbs 2:7 NLT; Proverbs 10:13 NLT; Proverbs 23:13-14 MSG)!

No discipline is enjoyable while it is happening—it's unpleasant and it is painful! However, while not societally sound, done properly, with the assured accompanied infusion of God's Word, there will be a peaceful harvest of right living for those who are trained in this way (Hebrews 12:11 NLT; Proverbs 22:15 AMP).

If you haven't already discerned—yes, I am a firm believer of the branch and staff method or modern translation—the belt—however, each child is different and the goal is not to punish, it is to inspire growth and maturity. While ADHD is indeed a real and very serious problem, many symptoms of A-D-H-D, in my opinion, can be cured by the B-E-L-T!!! The rest by God's W-O-R-D!!! Lack of God's Word breeds a deficiency in a child's development. This absence perpetuates the already established unruliness within a child's spirit and ossifies the waywardness in their soul!

Hebrews 4:12 sounds even more powerful than any stripes a belt could inflict when viewed in this light. Instead of outside in, the Word works inside out. Fathers are pointedly told not to provoke their children to anger (as punishment often does by engendering a negative response), but to bring them up in the discipline and instruction of the Lord (Ephesians 6:4). This "instruction of the Lord" is found in God's Word, your Mark of Authority! Your job as a Parent is not to abuse, nor to control your child. It is instead to nurture and instruct your child in such a way as to teach your child how to control itself.

Punishment and Discipline tread on fine lines, but, just like belief and Faith, are not interchangeable. Punishment is a parameter of control where the proverbial line is drawn with a "Don't do this or else" decree. Discipline introduces motives for change to better one's self. Personal responsibility is developed when boundaries and expectations are instituted and enforced. These disciplines are channels for growth, unlike punishments which are strictures and nondescript regulators. Punishments are challenges to get around while discipline invites awareness of self and personal accountability.

To illustrate the differences between both approaches, let's use something as benign as a cup of spilled milk. Little Tyler has been warned not to take his cup from the kitchen to the living room, but he continues to do so. This time he spills his milk. The Punishment Method would possibly comprise several factors—beginning with a rant, something along the lines of "How many times have I told you..." and ending with a "Go to your room!"—ensuring the behavior will continue without rhyme or reason where the child is concerned! After all, in the child's mind it's just spilt milk for crying out loud!

However, the Process of Discipline is preceded by parameters and comes to fruition through consequences as well as possible rewards. With the same scenario, Tyler has already been told under no circumstances is his cup to leave the kitchen, as well as the reasons behind this decree. Under the rules of this directive, if he brings his cup out of the kitchen and spills it, he will have to be responsible for his actions by cleaning the spill, as well as perhaps the whole room if the behavior continues (i.e. the spill, vacuuming the carpet, dusting the furniture and other mundane tasks).

The bottom line, making the mess dictates personal responsibility for the mess and therefore rectification of the mess. Depending on how young Tyler is, it may seem like an adventure to him at first due to its novelty, but I can assure you, Tyler will eventually get tired of it when he realizes EACH TIME HE WILL BE RESPONSIBLE TO CLEAN IT, NOT MOM, DAD, OR AN OLDER SIBLING.

In contrast, when Tyler shows good judgment by following the path of obedience and leaves his cup in the kitchen as instructed, his reward should not be tangible, but a far greater intangible foundation of moral character building of which you reinforce with praise and appreciation for his good judgment and respect for authority in obeying the established instructions.

Although not an immediate physical reward, it is a far better and more lasting building block that will in time produce good character and ethical stature. This ability to govern and navigate the road of one's own choices and therefore influence the outcome, builds courage and strength of character in your child. This also helps to slay the narcissistic tendencies of the flesh and focuses direction in obtaining goals.

Discipline makes the child aware of other's needs, as well as other's worth beyond his or her own (2 Corinthians 7). It also encourages the investment of your child in his or her own life while punishment forces a line towing mentality, which stunts creativity and stifles aggressive development of individual moral imperatives. In other words, Punishment and Discipline are the difference between a child waiting to be told what to do and one developing the ability, as well as the desire, of seeing a need and filling it properly without needing external direction!

Finally, the fourth way to Love your child is to say what you mean and mean what you say. Matthew 5:33-37 highlights the consequences of empty promises. Even though its original direction was to combat religious piety, it is definitely applicable in raising children because it reinforces the necessity of not falling into the trap of saying what you don't mean. You only make things worse when you lay down a smoke screen of empty threats by saying, "If you don't do this or that, there will be consequences," and then never follow through with what you've said. Or saying, "We'll go get a treat after you finish your chores," and not mean it.

Your words become ineffective when you say things you don't mean to smooth the immediate way or to evade initial conflict. In making your words sound more earnest through threats or promises and not following through, they become empty, hollow and meaningless to your child. When you manipulate your child with your words to get your own way, you go wrong because you are systematically bringing about an eventual breakdown of total communication and a lack of trust in you as their authority. Be truthful, don't lie to your children, they are a part of you. When you lie to them, you lie to yourself (Ephesians 4:25 MSG).

Another issue which can accompany saying what you mean and meaning what you say, is the problem of saying YES—all—the—time! You may not verbally utter yes, but your actions do when you allow your child to manipulate you through tears, pouting or tantrums. Do not be the parent who neglects a very crucial vitamin in your child's diet. Author and family psychologist John Rosemond identifies it as Vitamin N and suggests you give your child a healthy dose of it daily! It is the word NO! *It will not kill them!* It will not stunt their growth, nor will it not scar them for life or demolish their self-esteem. Quite frankly, self-esteem is overrated any way!

Don't worry about your child's self-esteem! Instead, be more concerned about the training of their spirit. A trained spirit will bring about the fortification of their soul, so self-esteem with take care of itself. Not understanding boundaries can put their lives in danger, cause them to become emotionally bankrupt through a false sense of entitlement and poison the adventure of life through the alienation or misuse of people due to a misdirected focus on themselves alone (Proverbs 16:32; Proverbs 25:28). Your children are wonderful, but they are not the center of the Universe—God is! Keep Him in His proper place by not allowing your children to become your god instead.

God demands in Exodus 20:3 that we have no other gods before Him and reiterates in Exodus 20:5 to neither worship them nor serve other gods because He is a jealous, impassioned God and demands what is rightfully and uniquely His—our worship and our service. God promises to avenge the trespass of a parent's false worship toward their children or any kind, *on* their children, to the third and fourth generations.

Choosing to serve other gods (your children in this case), translates to God as hate for Him when He is the Only God worthy of worship and service. However, He promises to show a graciousness and steadfast lovingkindness for thousands of generations, to those who Love Him and keep His commandments (Exodus 20:6).

Many children have hard and disastrous lives because they were placed above God in their parents lives. Please *do not* make this horrific error in judgment or *repent right now* if you have been doing so (1 John 1:9). Loving your children means having them in their appropriate place, below God and under your God-directed authority. It is imperative your yes, mean yes. Not a yes dictated by your child's fleshly display of intrepid manipulation, but one in accordance to Truth found in God's Word, and back it up with corresponding actions. For instance, do not reward a misbehaving child with what they want because of their display of temper or manipulative tears.

Rewarding a child when they do not deserve it or have not earned it, takes away incentive. This also fosters in them a sense of entitlement and will fuel narcissistic tendencies, which could ultimately destroy them. Let your no, be no! Not a no that deflects or shuts down interaction because you are hurried or don't want to be bothered, but one that disciplines and instructs and is followed by the appropriate consequences or rewards.

Be bold in the Lord and the Power of His Might. Invite the input of His Word to bring your children up in courage and integrity. Write the Word daily on your heart. It begins with you! "Do as I say and not as I do" might sound catchy, but it reeks of hypocrisy! Don't be misled. You cannot mock the justice of God. Without divine intervention, you will in some way always harvest what you plant. Those who live only to satisfy their own sinful nature will harvest decay and death from that sinful nature. However, those who live to please the Spirit will harvest everlasting Life from the Spirit. Allow the Word of God to permeate your heart and redesign your soul (Galatians 6:7-8; Hebrews 4:12)!

When you get Truth inside of you, you will then be able to get that same Truth inside your children by living it out before them. You must also talk about the Word wherever you are, sitting at home or walking on the street. Talk about and instruct with God's Word from the time you get up in the morning to when you fall into bed at night. Have reminders of His Word all around you. Display It in your home and on your gates (Deuteronomy 6:6-9).

If you have unruly children, they will not be won to Christ by badgering them with soapbox sermons, but by their witnessing your sacrificed life. Yes, *give* them the word verbally, but *live out what you teach from the Word*—daily! This is not a call to mount a proverbial pulpit and preach down heaven, nor is it a petition to bombard your children with a bunch of lip service. This is a call to Life Service. The Power of God and His Word (not the Force) is with you! What your children see you do will far outweigh what they hear you say!

God has not given you a spirit of fear, but has given you the Power of Love, so do not be afraid if you are married to Love your mate. If you are not marred to your children's other parent and are at war, a cease fire is in order! Call a truce under the red banner of Christ's Blood! Whether *they* are saved or not, *you* can operate in Faith and invite God in to negotiate surrender of self and usher in the fruition of His Will! He has also given you the Power of a sound mind, so do not neglect to pray for your spouse or the other parent and your children, as you impart the Word into your children's lives. Also be diligent to discipline your children as they grow and mature. You are in charge—they—are—not! It's Okay not to know what to do. It's *not* Okay to *continue* in ignorance of God's Word. So study God's Word and impart *His* Knowledge to your children and encourage them to know God for themselves (2 Timothy 1:7, 2:15).

It will not happen automatically because you send them, or personally take them to church. It will not miraculously become a part of them because they read a few Bible verses in Sunday School. They need to see it modeled out in real life. This is your call as their parent. The Word becomes real to your children when they see *He* is real in you. This is Faith's framework for Loving your children. This Love is already in you as God's Word Empowers you! Let go of what you know and allow God to work through you to empower your Family's Legacy for His Glory and for your children's good!

Chapter Fourteen

PUPPY LOVE

Do not give that which is holy to dogs,
and do not throw your pearls before pigs,
for they will trample them under their feet,
and turn and tear you to pieces.
~ Matthew 7:6 (AMP)

P uppy Love is an informal term for feelings of love, romance, or infatuation. Webster's Dictionary defines it as transitory love or affection felt during childhood and adolescence. It is named for its resemblance to the adoring, worshipful affection that may be felt by a puppy. Canadian singer Paul Anka helped to popularize it with his released single *Puppy Love* in 1960. It's obviously a popular term because several recording artists over the years also released songs with this title and most people are universally familiar with its meaning.

Puppy Love in and of itself is not bad. It can be beneficial when experienced through the filter of scriptural integrity. However, it is very destructive when experienced through the hipshot intemperance that flies in the face of conventional wisdom seen practiced in our world today. Webster's definition clearly focuses on child or adolescent affections when referring to Puppy Love. The targeted, erotic, and oft times pornographic images bombarding the youth of our nation is appalling and would have, only a few decades ago, landed the perpetrators of such lewdness on the social chopping block for its indecency and juvenile obtrusiveness.

The caviler way illicit sexual encounters have been glamorized into ostensibly hip, yet unpolished, terms like hook ups, booty calls and Netflix and chill, is testament to the fact this programing is wildly embraced by our nation's youth. How far our country has fallen from the temperate and virtuous ideologies on which she was founded! It is true America was not perfect in her inception, nor was she pure in her establishment. What does remain clear is that her foundation was set in Biblical Principles and was begotten by God's own intervention. Study history. Anyone can see America's formation was a miracle, an upstart nation with no real chance for a beginning, one doomed to failure and yet—she thrived. It had to be God. Why would He care? He took noticed because those who settled here called on His Name!

There used to be prayer and Bible based instruction in our public schools. The Ten Commandments hung proudly in every courthouse without contest and Merry Christmas was boldly proclaimed by well-wishers everywhere. How far we have fallen. As a nation we have forgotten our scriptural history, we have snubbed our Holy heritage and have lost our virtuous vision. Where there is no revelation of God and His Word, the people perish through a lack of inhibitions and unrestraint. Happy and blessed are those who adhere to the Word and Wisdom of God (Proverbs 29:18 AMP).

Our 44th President Barack Obama said, "We, the People, recognize that we have responsibilities as well as rights; that our destinies are bound together; that a freedom which only asks what's in it for me, a freedom without a commitment to others, a freedom without love or charity or duty or patriotism, is unworthy of our founding ideals, and those who died in their defense."

Unfortunately, this unworthiness is being personified! People are unrestrained and have no care for self or others when they do not know Truth. It is absolutely clear that God has called us to a free life. He did not give you free will only to cage you with religious dogmas and uptight legalism. He wants you to be a good citizen and respect the authorities. Whatever their level, they are God's emissaries for keeping order. It is God's Will that by doing good you might cure the ignorance of thickheaded people who think as a Christian, you're a danger to society (1 Peter 2:16 MSG).

Exercise your freedom by serving God, not by breaking the rules. Treat everyone you meet with dignity. Love your spiritual family. Revere God. Respect the government. Make sure that you don't use this freedom as an excuse to do whatever you want to do because being uncontrolled will inevitably destroy your freedom. We are instead to use our freedom to serve one another in Love. Everything we know about God's Word is summed up in a single sentence: *Love others as you Love yourself.* To do so is an act of true freedom. If we bite and ravage each other, it won't be long before we are obliterating one another, and where will our precious freedom be then? (1 Peter 2:17 MSG; Galatians 5:13-15 AMP).

The call to Love imparts direction and communicates vision. Habakkuk 2:2 commands, *"Write the vision, and make it plain upon tables, that he may run that reads it"* (NKJV). The Message Bible says to, *"write it out in block letters so it can be read on the run!"* This sounds like a billboard to me! So, think of the following as a billboard straight from God's Word to bless the rest of your life, as He prayerfully settles deep within your heart. May it be imbedded so profoundly that you spread it throughout your environment effortlessly, through words as well as actions and deeds; impacting all who encounter you, for the good of all, and for the Glory of God. People need to know that without Biblical Direction, the unrestrained lack of mental and emotional sobriety associated with Puppy Love, can lead to—a dog's life.

A Dog's Life

Dogs are a polygamous lot. They have no pair bonding or the protection of a single mate, but rather have multiple mates in a year. Dogs maximize the procreation of pups, which are then cared for by the mother alone. The pups rely on her for milk and protection and have no help or direction from the father. A dog's life was never God's plan for humanity. The Word of God tells us emphatically to run from sexual sin because no other sin so clearly affects the body as this one does. Sexual immorality is a sin against your own body. God commands us to honor marriage and guard the sacredness of sexual intimacy between **wife** and **husband** (1 Corinthians 6:18; Hebrews 13:4).

Boyfriend and girlfriend are not biblical terms, nor are they hinted at or alluded to in the biblical record in any favorable way. God draws a firm line against casual and illicit sex. We are reminded that because cities like Sodom and Gomorrah and their neighboring towns were filled with immorality and every kind of sexual perversion, the literal fire of God's Wrath destroyed them. This is to serve as a warning that the eternal fire of God's Judgment will come against those indulging in abhorrent immoral choices, unnatural vice and sensual perversity (Jude 1:7 AMP).

Shun a dog's life and embrace the Life God has for you! The key is to *Love yourself*. Not for the sake of self, but confidence in knowing God made you with purpose! American singer and guitarist George Benson released a hit back in 1977, composed by Michael Masser (music) and Linda Creed (lyrics) which proclaimed *The Greatest Love of All* is learning to Love yourself. Actually, the Bible reveals that the Greatest Love is to Love The Lord your God with all your passion and prayer and intelligence and energy. The second is to Love others as well as you Love yourself (Mark 12:30, 31 MSG).

Only then, through the knowledge of the Truth (studying God's Word), will you be able to Love yourself and therefore Love others. Without God's Word, without Truth to guide and Love to light the path of life, the only thing left to do is stumble around in the dark of our own tainted imaginations, blinded by the grasping insatiability of our ignoble natures. This is why the god of this world campaigns so strongly through the fallen heart of man to convince anyone listening that we have no worth, no intrinsic value. The crusades to place animals, the environment and any other thing above human life is an insidious ploy to pull the wool over the eyes of your understanding and impair the ears of your reason so you miss the fact that Love says you have worth and Love says you have value! God's Word reveals to each man the vision of his worth and to each woman the vision of her value!

His Worth

God formed the Man out of dirt from the ground and blew into his nostrils the breath of life, so when Man came alive he was a living soul, an individual complete in body and spirit! God then created a Garden encompassing what was needed for the Man to thrive before placing the Man there to labor and watch over it. In order for the Man to exercise his free will, God gave him only one command. He could eat from any tree in the garden except from the Tree-of-Knowledge-of-Good-and-Evil. He emphatically told the Man not to eat from it because the moment he did eat from that tree, he would die (Genesis 2:7-17).

I'm sure you know the story well. He ate and the consequence of disobedience manifested in a curse to fall on all of humanity! The ground was also cursed because of the Man's disobedience. Whereas before his sin, the Man's labor had been easy and joyous; after sin, getting food from the ground was sorrowful and full of drudgery because he had to work harder to plant, till and harvest. The ground did not just yield to him it's harvests as it had done before it was cursed. God told the Man that he would sweat in the fields from dawn to dusk, until he returned to that ground, dead and buried. God also reminded the Man that he started out as dirt and he'd end up dirt. Starting out as dirt may seem like a negative, but it was not. God made Man out of what He later gave him authority over—the Whole Earth (Geneses 3:9-11, 17-19; Genesis 1:26)!

Man's worth to God is so high that He entrusted Man with the whole earth! This is why before sin, the earth yielded to the Man willingly and with minimal effort on the Man's part. God set up the whole earth in difference to the Man. Man had dominion and authority, which is also why God tasked him to name the animals (Genesis 2:19). Man's choice to sin gave the birthright that was given to him by God, over to the devil and placed division between himself and his wife.

From the first day judgment for the Man's sin was imputed upon him to this day, Man still has to rigorously labor to forge out a living. If you are a man, the joy of your salvation is that the Law of the Spirit of Life in Christ has *FREED* you from the judgment meted out for the first Man's sin! You are free! This is what Salvation means. Freedom! You no longer have to toil in sorrow with little yield! God has restored Eden to you! As a Man of God, your worth is assured and your favor intact! The Authority given away has been restored!

The earth is the Lord's and the fullness thereof and He has restored this Authority back to you through the Glory of His Salvation and by the Power vested in you through His Son Jesus! Seek God for your purpose and not what the world says makes you man, like seeking pleasures of the flesh. Don't be like the prodigal son who squandered his inheritance with undisciplined and dissipated living (Psalm 24:1; 2 Thessalonians 2:14; 1 Corinthians 15:57; Luke 15:11-32).

Single or married, sexual conquests do not define manhood, self-control does. Allowing intemperance to reign is like an unsecured house in the middle of the Hood! No alarm system, unlocked doors and wide open windows invites the plunderous theft of your goods and vandal's imaginative defacement of your walls!

What happens when you live God's way? He brings gifts into your life, much the same way that fruit appears in an orchard. Where intemperance dismantles virtue, self-control amplifies qualities like affection for others, exuberance about life and tranquility. You'll develop a willingness to stick with things, a sense of compassion in the heart, and a conviction that even the most basic holiness causes to permeate things and people. You'll find yourself involved in loyal commitments, not needing to force your way in life, as well as able to marshal and direct your energies wisely (Proverbs 25:28; Titus 1:8; Galatians 5:22-23 MSG).

If you are single, keeping yourself whole and pure before God is a necessity to receive God's Best for you. If you are married, fidelity to your wife translates into blessings for your soul and contributes favorably toward matrimonial cohesiveness. Do not allow the enemy to rob you of your inheritance as God's child. ___You have worth___ so Love yourself by sanctifying yourself for God. You are a vessel for the Holy Spirit so do not scatter your inheritance to the wind! Also, if you have established covenants, do not fool yourself into thinking that you are not responsible for them.

They do not evaporate especially if progeny have resulted. Stand up in who you are as a man, repent and accept responsibility! Ask God for direction and keep your eyes focused on His Word. Hold tight to your convictions in Christ! Give following God's Ways all you've got, be resolute! Put away lust and instead, Love without apprehension or restraint!

Her Value

After everything was established, named and settled, God saw it was not good for the Man to be alone and decided to make a help and a companion fit for Him. God put the Man into a deep sleep. As he slept, God removed one of his ribs and replaced it with flesh. God then used the rib that he had taken from the Man to make Woman and presented her to the Man. After the Woman's choice to disobey, a war was declared between the devil and the Woman. This war is one of the reasons women are so objectified and exploited across the world. The curse also decreed that the Woman's pains in childbirth would be multiplied and the desire to control her husband would plague her even though her husband would still have authority over her (Genesis 2:18-25; 3:15-16).

If you are a woman, the joy of your salvation is that the Law of the Spirit of Life in Christ has also *FREED* you from the judgment meted out for the first Woman's sin! You are free! This is what Salvation means. Freedom!

The Woman was inside of man at the time of his creation, Genesis 1:28 reads, *"So God created Man in His own image, in the image of God created He him; male and female created He them"* because of this fact, the Woman is afforded the same authority over earth as the man. Their worth is equal and therefore, their inheritance through Christ is identical. *How* she was created makes a difference in *who* she is, and Her *value* is also different because of her *role* in God's established order, but neither factor diminishes her worth to God. Man came from hard ground and woman came from bone protected by soft flesh. Here marks a physical difference in the sexes!

God's Word notes the difference and states although she is *physically* weaker, as a woman she is to be shown honor *and* respect as a *fellow heir* to the Grace of Life (1Peter 3:7). If you are female, in Christ you no longer have to endure multiplied pain in childbirth or desire to usurp your husband's authority or compete with the male ego! God has restored Eden to you! There is no need for the Betty Hutton/Howard Keel type rivalry as a Woman of God because your worth is assured, and your favor intact! The Authority given away has been restored!

If you are married, you are in equal standing and are a complement to your husband. If you are single, you have been given a very unique and highly significant assignment as God's daughter to live a full life, not inferior to, nor in competition with Man.

You are Woman! Out of you comes heritage, through you flows life and with you covenant is established. You do not have to actually birth children to be a Mother to many and as a daughter of destiny, you are a sentinel of covenant, a guardian of sealed agreement! God remembers covenant forever, for a thousand generations! He does not take covenant lightly! The covenant of our salvation was secured by Christ's sacrifice, but it was through the shedding of His blood that eternal covenant was sealed and ratified. This authorization equips us with every good thing to carry out God's Will for our lives (Psalm 105:8; Hebrews 13:20-21).

Virginity is sacred because the shedding of blood establishes covenant. God does not call you to purity for His sake; He calls you to purity for your own. When virginity is treated as if it does not matter (male or female virginity), this flies in the face of God's established law, instituted for your *protection* (Hebrews 13:4 AMP). As Psalm 105:8 testifies that God remembers covenant forever, wouldn't you want God to remember something that actually matters and not something established on a whim; because it's Prom night and others are doing it or because you think you are in love right now or to keep a boyfriend?

The wise Woman builds her life on a foundation of Godly precepts, and in so doing, her life will thrive. But the foolish one who lacks spiritual insight, tears it down with her own hands by ignoring Godly-principles. A beautiful woman who is without discretion is like a gold ring in the snout of a pig. A Woman's lack of character invalidates whatever beauty she has (Proverbs 14:1; Proverbs 11:22 AMP).

You have value! Your worth is not just because you are one of God's uniquely precious jewels, but also because you establish covenant! It is important to not form covenant without lawful commitment. If you've already done so, ask God to forgive your ignorance and trust that He'll restore you back to Himself, then make up your mind to keep yourself, through His Word and Grace. If it was stolen from you without consent, know that God can heal your heart and free you of the hurt, rage and shame you may still feel through a Spirit of forgiveness. You are very precious to God. His Word is for your protection and for you to understand who you are to Him. You are not an abandoned building where squatters take ease and vandals hide. Choose to Love yourself by sanctifying yourself for God. Self-respect is an automatic incentive for others to respect you in turn. You are a vessel for the Holy Spirit, so guard your gates! *__You have value;__* therefore, you are *worth* the price of admission!

Chapter Fifteen

LET'S TALK ABOUT SEX

Honor marriage, and guard the sacredness of sexual intimacy between wife and husband. God draws a firm line against casual and illicit sex.
~ Hebrews 13:4 (MSG)

Do not be deceived! Sex is not a four-letter word (after all it only has three letters)! It is not a dirty, undercover secret, nor a back-door rebellion (puns intended)! Sex was God's idea from the beginning. He invented it and He created male and female anatomically to perform and revel in it. When He told Adam and Eve to be fruitful, to multiply and to replenish the Earth, believe me, He was not sending them off to solve a bunch of mathematical equations or to plant a bunch of fruit trees (Genesis 1:28)! He meant S-E-X and having babies!

Sex is not and has *never* been a problem for God. He is not uptight or squeamish, nor is He off somewhere blushing in a corner when people talk about sex. All those naysayers who allude to the specious position that He is against sex are either deceived, or are grasping at a thin air excuse to continue in their depravity or—and you guessed it—they are trying to sell you something! Don't buy the lie anymore! Everything God does has a purpose and a meaning. The problem with sex is not sex itself—it is *how* sex is used.

For example, take slam dunking a basketball. A player has a beeline, wide-open drive straight down center court, alley-oop to his teammate and swish—nothing but net! Nothing wrong with that, right? Well let's move the same scenario to a kitchen. One child has a beeline, wide-open drive straight down the center of the kitchen island, alley-oop to his brother and swish—into the huge steam pot full of crab legs on the stove! Totally inappropriate, right? Also, I think their Mother would have a big problem with that! Be assured, our Heavenly Father has a huge problem with inappropriately using what He intended for good, as well!

It is not the action, but the incongruous application of the action itself is where God's issue resides. God created sex for marriage and marriage only! 1 Corinthians 7:2 encourages each man to have his *own* wife and each woman to have her *own* husband in order to avoid sexual immorality. I think it is telling how the Bible stresses "own" in the scripture. Own meaning no one else's husband or wife! A bold and unfortunately needed clarification to avoid any misunderstandings!

The husband should fulfill his wife's sexual needs and the wife should fulfill her husband's sexual needs as well. God never intended sex to be abused nor withheld. He is clear that the wife is to give authority over her body to her husband and that the husband reciprocates and gives authority over his body to his wife. There is nothing to limit their exploration of one another, nor in taking joy in each another. Basically, anything goes because of God's immense Generosity and Grace (1 Corinthians 7:3-4)

Dissection and scrutinizing of every action to see if it is permissible is not necessary as long as the activity in which a husband and his wife engage is only between one another, violates none of God's precepts and are of mutual consent. A husband and wife are not to deprive one another of sexual relations unless they both agree to refrain from sexual intimacy with each other for a limited time in order to fast and to pray (and of course for medical reasons, i.e. after the birth of a child, surgery etc.). Afterward, they are commanded to come together again, so that satan won't be able to tempt them because of their need for sexual intimacy (1 Corinthians 10:23; 1 Corinthians 7:5). This is God's ideal.

As you know, this is not the world's standard by any means. Unfortunately, promiscuity has become a staple of our culture; a duplicitous rite of passage, as common as changing one's clothes. We have dressed up immorality like an elegant night out on the town instead of the garish parade that God says it is. We have relabeled debauchery to make it more palatable or politically correct. Adultery is now an affair, fornication is making love, and virginity is a noose to be removed from around one's neck post haste.

While we are indeed free moral agents, there are choices that give us good lives and choices that destroy lives. Sexual intemperance takes us down a path that weakens and dismantles the tenants for a good and productive life. There are a plethora of consequences emitting from this intemperate lifestyle choice. We tend to rally around the obvious ones like unwanted pregnancies, sexually transmitted diseases and the disintegration of families when adultery becomes known. However, one other such consequence that is chiefly overlooked is the development of an inability to properly connect with or to have empathy for people. The Bible calls it waxing cold.

Waxing Cold

My daughter's class executed a shockingly simple, yet profoundly memorable experiment that greatly personifies not only the need for purity in one's body as related to sexual intimacy for both sexes, but also as it relates to the ability to mentally and emotionally bond with another individual. Each child was given a strip of scotch tape about two inches in length and then instructed to place it on the inside of someone else's wrist, then another and then another. They soon found the adhesive properties of the tape to dramatically diminish after each removal, becoming nonexistent after a few times until it would eventually curl up or just fall off completely.

This simple experiment accurately demonstrates an inability to hold steadfast after several fleeting attempts at so called intimacy with others prior to marriage. Improper attachments make it more difficult to forge a proper bond with a mate and, as with any caged beast, once freed, it is indiscriminate with whom it attacks. When sin is rampant everywhere, the love of many will grow cold. Without divine intervention, this inability to bond is indiscriminate and transfers to everyone a person comes in contact with, in varying degrees. As Matthew 24:12 states:

"And because iniquity shall abound, the love
of many shall wax cold."

Of course, this scripture is talking about sin in general. However, we are specifically warned to run away from sexual immorality in any form, whether thought or behavior, whether visual or written because every other sin that one commits is outside the body, but the one who is sexually immoral sins against their own body. We are urged to abstain from these sensual urges and dishonorable desires because they wage war against our very soul (1 Corinthians 6:18; 1 Peter 2:11 AMP).

We unintentionally sign up to engage in this war when we deliberately disregard these warnings. The "iniquity" mentioned in Matthew 24:12, in the Greek is *anomia* (ä-no-mē>-ä) and means lawlessness, contempt and violation of law, wickedness. This is a *willful* violation of Truth. When we have contempt for and disregard what we know to be Truth in response to our baser nature, God calls this sin. The price is higher and the penalties steeper (James 4:17; Ezekiel 18:24).

This brings us to the result of the willful disregard of Truth, the penalty of waxing cold. "Wax cold" in the Greek is *psychō* (psü'-khō), yes PSYCHO! Look it up for yourself. I know I was floored!!! It means to be made cold or to grow cold, of disappearing love. Webster's definition of psycho is a psychopathic or psychotic person, one who is crazy or mentally unstable. Webster's goes on to describe a person with psychopathic tendencies as one who manifests amoral conduct, having or showing no concern about whether behavior is morally right or wrong as well as antisocial behavior that is hostile or harmful to organized society.

This person lacks the ability to love or establish meaningful interpersonal relationships, is extremely egocentric and fails to learn from experience. This means that no matter how damaging the results of this person's actions, they will continue to repeat the same actions which bring about the same detrimental results, over and over again!

Let's reread Matthew 24:12 with these characterizations in mind. "And because uncontrolled wickedness, the contempt and willful violation of God's Law is amplified, many people's ability to love will become nonexistent; resulting in a show of no concern about whether behavior is morally right or wrong, as well a rise in repetitively crazy or mentally unstable behavior that is hostile or harmful to the social order."

In light of this knowledge, the fact men are singularly targeted and encouraged to follow the sinister mindset of variety when it comes to sexual partners becomes clear. The resulting fallout produces men who are emotionally distant, antisocial and morally bankrupt! When the head is compromised, the household is in jeopardy! When women also fall prey to this reckless behavior, the whole concept of family is lost entirely! The redefining of gender roles, as well as the idea of gender itself, becomes a malleable concept under the onslaught of uncontrolled wickedness fueled by the willful contempt and reckless disregard of God's Law.

To willfully participate in sexual sin is to voluntarily invite mental, emotional and physical instability. This would account for the unexplainable irrationality of unrestrained humanity. Sin debilitates will and sexual sin annihilates reason. Sexual sin is insidious in its casualness, damaging in its execution and devastating by design. However, the mindset resulting from the fallout of dishonest sexual self-indulgence is even worse because it mimics an unrealized virus in the system of the subconscious. It creates a guilty cognizance that underlies everything a person involved in sexual sins does and can dictate this person's actions to the point that they really don't understand their own motives. The carnal nature is real, so real in fact that when we want to do what is right, we end up not doing it (Titus 1:15; Romans 7:15 AMP).

Instead, we do what we know is wrong, damaging and what we absolutely despise. We must place this wickedness before God because it is a secret sin we have tried to conceal with self-indulgent terms like enlightenment, modern times and freedom. The bottom line is that God sees it all for what it truly is, self-defacing and depraved. This outlook is not at the forefront of people's minds, but it is there. It is like a hidden piece of code in a computer system that hijacks the commands of the user and does what it was designed to do—steal, kill and destroy (Psalm 90:8; John 10:10 AMP).

It is a hook of the enemy. He knows we can't keep our true self hidden forever. Before long, we will be exposed! We cannot hide behind palatial monikers or religious masks forever. Eventually, the smoke will clear, the mirrors will shatter and the mask will slip, then our true face will be known. We cannot whisper one thing in private and speak the opposite in public. The day is coming when those whispers will be repeated so loud that everyone will know our business (Luke 12:2-3).

God's Word is very clear. He does not wink at or overlook sin. He is very displeased with the ungodliness and unrighteousness of people who in their wickedness suppress and stifle the Truth. God says to run away from youthful lusts and instead pursue righteousness, Faith, Love, and Peace with believers who call on the Lord out of a pure heart. Those who fail to believe and trust in Him are without excuse and without defense because God has made His requirements plain. When people know God as the Creator, but do not honor Him as God or give thanks for His wondrous creation, they become worthless in their thinking—godless! They soon give place to pointless reasoning and silly speculations. Deplorably so, that their foolish hearts are darkened (2 Timothy 2:22; Romans 1:18-21).

These people claim to be wise, but in consequence, they become fools and exchange the glory, majesty and excellence of the immortal God for worthless idols of self and inanimate things of no value. Therefore, God will give them over to the lusts of their own hearts and to sexual impurity, so that their bodies will be dishonored among them. They will be totally abandoned to the degrading power of sin. By choice, they exchanged the truth of God for a lie, and worshiped and served the creature rather than the Creator. In refusing to know God, they soon will no longer know how to be human either. Women won't know how to be women and men won't know how to be men. Sexually confused, they'll abuse and defile one another, women with women, men with men—all lust and no Love (Romans 1:22-27).

Since they do not see fit to acknowledge God or consider Him worth knowing as their Creator, they pay dearly. Emptied of God and Love, they become godless and loveless wretches because God has given them over to a depraved mind, to do things which are improper and repulsive, until they were filled, permeated and saturated with every kind of unrighteousness (Romans 1:28). Sexual sin is a sign of an inward lack. There is a God sized whole inside of every one of us. God placed it there for Himself and *ONLY* He can fill this place.

His Temple

You need to realize that your body is a sacred place, the place designed to indwell God's very Spirit. No one will get by with vandalizing God's Sacred Place, you can be sure of that. God's Temple is sacred and you, *are* His Temple. It is imperative you understand that living however you please has great consequences (1 Corinthians 3:16-17). When you squander what God paid such a high price for, it is impossible to receive the Best God has for you in this state.

Before Salvation, you were held hostage to a sinful nature and you were prey for a sinful society. By accepting Christ, the huge sum that was paid out for your ransom through His Ultimate Sacrifice, was applied to your life. If you were living a Dogs' Life, please don't choose out of habit to continue doing what society tells you is correct by incorrectly defining your manhood or your womanhood, outside of God's Perfect Design for your life. The physical part of you is not a piece of property you own apart from the spiritual part of you. God owns the whole works, so let people see God in and through you. Especially in how you care for your body, as well as your soul and spirit (1 Corinthians 6:19, 20; 1 Corinthians 7:23AMP).

God wants you to live a pure life and to keep yourself from sexual promiscuity. This is not to kill your fun or to wreck your good time, but to preserve your soul! The integrity of self protects your mind and your body, as well as positions you for all the blessings He has set up for you to receive. Liberating decrees like The Emancipation Proclamation have nothing on what the freeing Power of Grace has done for your life! Learn to appreciate and give dignity to your body by not abusing it, as is so common among those who know nothing of God or His Ways. You have no obligation to do what your old iniquitous nature urges you to do. In Christ, that part of you is dead anyway, drowned under the Blood of Jesus so it does not get a vote unless you allow it a seat at the table (1 Thessalonians 4:3-5)!

If you do allow its cheyne stoking entry and choose to live by its dishonorable dictates, you will not inherit God's Kingdom (more on this in the next chapter). However, if through the Power of the Spirit you put to death the deeds of your old sinful nature, you will live. For all who are led by the Spirit of God are the children of God. You have not received a spirit that makes you a fearful slave to your baser needs. Instead, you received God's Spirit when He adopted you as His own child (Romans 8:12-15 MSG).

This means killing off everything connected with the ways of death: sexual promiscuity, impurity, lust, doing whatever you feel like whenever you feel like it, and gravitating to the Way of the Lord for cleansing, empowerment and freedom.

Divine Purpose

There's more to sex than mere skin on skin. Sex is as much a spiritual mystery as a physical fact. It is written in Scripture, *"The two become one"* (Mark 10:8). As Believers, we want to become spiritually one with God, so we must not pursue the kind of sex that avoids commitment and intimacy because in the end these casual hook ups, malfeasant and adulterous lesions leave us lonelier than ever. This happens because it is the kind of sex that can never "become one" as God intend through the marriage bond. Remember, sexual sins are different from all other sins. In sexual sin, the sacredness of your own body is violated. Your body was made for God-given and God-modeled expressions of Love, for "becoming one" with a spouse in requisite commitment (1 Corinthians 6:18-20 MSG).

Going back to the slam dunk example, a basketball was made for a basketball hoop! This was its design. It can be used to dunk other places, but in the end all that remains will be a mess to clean up! Take owning a snowmobile for another example. The snowmobile was designed to cover great distances sleekly and swiftly over snow covered terrains. Riding your snowmobile on the bare asphalt will destroy the rubber shielding the tracks, as well as the rub bars covering the skies. To use your snowmobile during the wrong season, like summer, where there are no snow covered terrains, will cause damage that otherwise would not be incurred if used during a proper season like Winter, when the ground is covered with snow. Sex has a proper season. It's called marriage and to use it in any other season will incur damage.

Also, keep in mind that covenant is established when blood is shed. When virginity is taken or given freely without the benefit of marriage, it is in effect stolen or commandeered from the eventual covenant to be established between the husband and wife. God Calls this a transgression. In this matter of sexual misconduct, God says no man shall go beyond and defraud his brother (Hebrews 9:18; 1 Thessalonians 4:6 AMP).

For a man (or woman) to "go beyond" in the Greek is *hyper-bainō* (hü-per-bī'-nō) and means to overstep the proper limits, trespass, do wrong, sin. It also goes on to state that the one who does this is defrauding another in a business transaction. Webster defines covenant as an agreement, a legal contract. The Bible solemnly warns that the Lord is the Avenger in all these things for God has not called us to impurity, but to holiness. Holiness means to be dedicated and set apart by behavior that pleases Him, whether in public or in private. So, if you reject and disregard this, you are not rejecting man, but the God who gives His Holy Spirit to you to dwell in you and empower you to overcome temptation (1 Thessalonians 4:6-8). This is a twofold transgression!

The first is a desecration of covenant and the second is against God Himself! When you put yourself and your needs before God, the Bible calls this idolatry! In worshiping yourself as your own god, you at the same time pull yourself away from your only Source of Love—God! The Bible is firm in relaying that God is a jealous God and demands no other gods get put before Him. This includes yourself. This is a Dog's life, a life shaped by things and feelings instead of by the Eternal Wisdom imparted by God (Colossians 3:5-8; Jonah 2:8; Exodus 20:3 AMP).

Loving yourself means you must not give sin a vote in the way you conduct your life. Don't give evil the time of day. Don't even run little errands that relate to that old way of life. Remember, when you accepted Christ as Savior, you took on His Spirit, so you are no longer dead in trespasses and sins! You are now alive through Him, so throw yourself wholeheartedly and full-time into God's Way of doing things. He has given you authority over and protection from every assault of the enemy. Nothing can harm you. This is the you that matters—the eternal you! Physical, emotional and mental hurts may come but sin can no longer tell you how to live because you are no longer living under the old tyranny of sin's power. You're now living in a freedom that only God can provide (Luke 10:19AMP; Romans 6:12-14 MSG).

If you are male and have transgressed against God's conventional law by establishing one or several unlawful covenants please be aware, you are called to a higher Life in Him! He will forgive and deliver you! If you are female and have established an unlawful covenant by consensually giving away your virginity, or if it was stolen from you without such consent, God can heal your heart and deliver you as well! Please say the next words OUT LOUD and claim the territory and victory God says is yours through His Son.

"Father God, I come before you, acknowledging that I have placed ungodly wants and desires before You. I ask that you forgive me and deliver me from the snares of my flesh and the wrong ways in my mind. I no longer want to live by my feelings and want You in Your right place as Lord over my life and my body. Show me daily how to please You with my whole self: spirit, soul and body from this day forward. I give You me. Thank You for delivering me and helping me be sensitive to The Holy Spirit's Direction and restore me back to You. In Jesus' Name ~ Amen!"

If you believe what you just spoke out loud, YOU ARE DELIVERED! All you must do now is walk in the deliverance and Power afforded you in Christ. This may seem a daunting task, but fear not, God is here for you. He has not given you a spirit of timidity, cowardice or fear, but He has given you a Spirit of Power and of Love and of Sound Judgment and Personal Discipline. This Empowerment generates abilities that result in a calm spirit, a well-balanced mind and the Power to control yourself (2 Timothy 1:7 AMP)!

There will never be a test or temptation that will confront you that is beyond the course of what others have had to face. Always remember that it is intemperance that makes you a slave to your passions, but self-control gives you the freedom and power of choice! Freedom is not tossing off common decency. It is empowered by holding fast to values indigenous to moral character (1 Corinthians 10:13; Romans 7:14-25 AMP).

It is the *secular* authorities that tell you sexual inactivity will hurt you physically and emotionally. God fearfully and wonderfully made you, so it's safe not to accept this supposition as fact. He knows how you work better than the most informed physician. All you need to remember is that God will never let you down. He'll never let you be pushed past your limit. He'll always be there to help you come through it, IF (and notice that is a BIG *"IF"*) you put your Faith and Trust in *Him* and not your own ability (Psalm 100:3; Psalm 139:14; 1 Corinthians 10:13; Proverbs 3:5) .

I am reminded of a documentary chronicling an incident a few years back that took place a couple counties over from mine in which several teenagers were affected by a syphilis epidemic. Evidently, these teens were participating in huge orgy style circles of friends with benefits over several months and this all became known when the syphilis outbreak could not be contained. The documentary followed several of these teens in the aftermath of their devastating choices. One among these Teens quite broke my heart.

He repented and asked Jesus into his heart and had been trying to turn his life around for a couple months and was having a really hard time. You see, the desires and appetites he'd awakened within himself were still there. He was trying, through sheer force of will, to contain or disband them. People prayed for him and with him, but nothing seemed to work for this young man. He eventually walked away from his fledgling faith. He walked away because he didn't know what was right or true. He went back into captivity because he had no knowledge (Matthew 15:14; Proverbs 19:2 AMP; Hosea 4:6; Isaiah 5:13).

The body has an excellent memory! What you have trained it to do, it will crave to do. If you have had an active illicit sex life, just because you prayed, don't think those desires are just going to go away overnight—get real! Don't get me wrong, God is Awesome. He may choose to deliver you with the snap of a finger, but if He does not, don't get discouraged. As with anything worthwhile, it may not come easy, but when it comes, it will be greater appreciated and will come swifter when you rely upon God for Support. You can do everything through Christ who gives you the strength to do so (Philippians 4:13).

I remember when I was one hundred pounds overweight! That is to say, when I finally *realized* I was that huge and decided to lose weight. The weight didn't just fall off overnight! No matter how hard I cried or prayed. The weight didn't move until I changed my choices! Choose this day forward to make better choices. Yes, pray and cry if necessary, but even though God didn't take you by the hand and guide you into sexual promiscuity, trust Him and He *will* take you by the hand and guide you out of it.

Just as the correct choices in self-delay, culinary options and exercise saw the steady depletion of the circumference of my waist, hips and thighs, so too will the heavy weight of dishonest sexual desire lessen as you reach for more of Christ. This is Faith's framework for having a fulfilled life. By following God's Plan you are cleansed, you are made Holy and you are made right with Him by calling on the Name of Jesus Christ, following the Way of the Word and being led by the Spirit of God. This empowers you to not only properly Love others, but first and foremost, to properly Love yourself (Philippians 4:19; Zechariah 4:6c; 1 Corinthians 6:9-11 MSG).

Chapter Sixteen

INHERITANCE

I know what I'm doing. I have it all planned out—
plans to take care of you, not abandon you,
plans to give you the future you hope for.
~ God (Jeremiah 29:11 MSG)

I love the old Gospel hymn *His Eye is on The Sparrow*, written in 1905 by lyricist Civilla D. Martin and composer Charles H. Gabriel. It eloquently begins with "Why should I feel discouraged..." and triumphantly ends with "His eye is on the sparrow, and I know He watches me."

When you are assured of God's Love and Protection, there is very little to cause you discouragement. Worry, doubt and distress all lead to discouragement and have their root in fear! Fear is a spirit and according to 2 Timothy 1:7, *"God has not given you a spirit of timidity, cowardice or fear but He has given you a Spirit of Power and of Love and of Sound Judgment as well as personal discipline resulting in abilities that produce a calm, well-balanced mind and self-control"* (AMP). He has also given you Authority over evil, and the ability to exercise authority over all the power of your adversary the devil, so that nothing will in any way harm you (Luke 10:19).

This authority from God is yours and supersedes all else, but this only happens if you choose to walk *in* this God-authored and God-ordained Authority. Look at it this way, let's say you are a homeowner and have the Rolls Royce equivalent of homeowner's insurance available in your area. There is no out of pocket deductible required and the premiums are paid in full! A perfect position to be in when a storm comes and when it does, it's a Euroclydon of Biblical proportions! Once the storm ends you find there is extensive damage to your house and many repairs are needed.

However, because you didn't look at the fine print or know your rights set by the validity of your contract, you disregard contacting your insurance company to notify them of the damage. Instead of acquiring the facts, you decide to run around like your neighbors are doing, trying to take care of the repairs yourself because you believe, like your radically underinsured neighbors, that you can get everything done cheaper than your deductible would cost—totally oblivious to the fact your deductible has already been taken care of!

When the time, energy, effort and expense decidedly overwhelm you and you're at the whit's end of exhaustion, you finally humble yourself and call The Company! When you call in an impatient temper expecting immediate results, you totally miss the fact that had you called The Company in the first place you'd most likely be at the end of all repairs and satisfied with the results. Instead, you're basically still at the beginning, having wasted a lot of your time, energy and effort to no avail because The Company now has to transform your chaos into the correct outcome.

This is what we do with God. Jesus paid it all! Whatever you are into that needs resolution, God has provided the answer or the way of escape! No test or temptation that comes your way is beyond the course of what others have had to face. All you need to remember is that God will never let you down. He will deliver you from every evil attack when you rely upon Him. He Knows how to rescue His people from trials or equip you as you go through them. He will never let you be pushed past your limit and will always be there to help you come through whatever is seeking to overtake you (1 Corinthians 10:13; 2 Timothy 4:18; 2 Peter 2:9).

If you have been saved for a while, have you found many times you feel you can handle whatever "it" is on your own, only to find yourself having go to God with whatever "it' is when you realize you cannot? If you've recently committed your life to Christ, I want you to know He Is a Safe Place to hide, ever present and ready to Help, when you need Him (Psalm 46:1).

Make the decision right now to STOP! Just stop doing things your way or worse, doing things the way you've seen others do them when you know their way does not line up with God's Way or ultimately produces dissolute consequences or haphazard results! Think about it! Has this way gotten you the outcomes you wanted? The way of life that you've led thus far looked harmless enough, but please look again. Is it leading you away from God's Will and purposes? Are you merely towing some line of religious piety? Are you just going with the flow of other's expectations? It may seem as though you were having a good time, but all that laughter eventually ended in heartbreak, right (Isaiah 55:8; Proverbs 14:12, 13 MSG)? Remember, you have what would be considered the Rolls Royce of insurances as a child of the Most High God! There is not an out of pocket deductible required and the premiums have been paid in full by Christ Jesus, so choose now to do it God's Way and watch Him work things out for you. Again, that Way, that Path is the road choosing to Love.

Family Tree

You did not get to choose your biological parents, siblings or extended family. You were born into all the practical pitfalls and pervasive idiosyncrasies that accompany these inherited, interpersonal entanglements. It can be humbly honorable or indecently nefarious, either way, we tidily call it family. Whether nuclear, single-parent, composite, adopted, blended or extended, regardless of the kind of family you hail from, being in it was not the result of your own choosing. You are therefore not entitled to all the accolades if your family is noteworthy, nor are you responsible to shoulder the blame if it is not. Exodus 34:7 in the Amplified essentially states that God will keep mercy and lovingkindness for thousands, forgiving iniquity and transgression and sin. However, He will by no means leave the guilty unpunished, avenging the sin and guilt of fathers upon their children and their grandchildren to the third and fourth generations by calling their children to account for the sins of their fathers.

Upon first reading this, it would seem God is being unjust. Where is the justice in a child paying for what his or her lineage did before their conception?! Exactly! There is no justice in this, which is why He sent His Son! Remember, Romans 8:2 proclaims that the law of the Spirit of Life, which is in Christ Jesus, has made you free from the law of sin and death, of which generational curses are a part. Outside of Christ, you are bound to the law of sin and death, the sin and guilt of your ancestry would be upon you, your children and their grandchildren to the third and fourth generations. However, as God's child, through accepting all Christ has done for you, you are now free from the generational curses and offenses consequential to this declared end. You have the Rolls Royce of earthly and eternal insurances through Christ Jesus! All you must do now is walk in it!

Love dictates that you walk in all God has sacrificed for you to have. He sacrificed His Dear Son so that you might Live! This is how much God Loves you! This is how you can have victory and not be destroyed. By believing in and being obedient to Him, you can have a whole and everlasting life. God did not go through all the heartbreak and sacrifice of sending His only begotten Son merely to point an accusing finger telling you how bad you are or to berate you for whatever messed-up bloodline you've descended. Jesus came to help you, to put your world right again. If you choose to trust Him, you are acquitted! If you refuse to trust Him, you remain beneath the death sentence of generational curses even though you are saved from the penalty of death (John 3:16-21).

Many Christians live ragledy lives, yes *rag-la-dee,* that's raggedy and lazy lives because they have no real hope for their future. Granted, they are saved and Heaven is their home, but they live hopeless, heartless and unfulfilled lives here on earth. Ask yourself, "Am I a person who says the right things to align myself with what would be considered proper Christian edict, but my heart really isn't in it?" Are you doing what you know is right to do, like going to church and even doing the work of ministry: singing in the Choir, teaching Sunday School or on the Usher Board or are even a Deacon or Minister, but somewhere along the way the real meaning of it is lost on your heart?

Have you found yourself using the things of God as a cover for doing whatever suits your fancy for the moment and in effect, ditching God's Command to do whatever you feel to do with the mentality that "God understands" or "He knows my heart"? This is the very definition of religion. Holding to a form of outward godliness when it is convenient, while at the same time denying its power, nullifies any real claim of faith (2 Timothy 3:5 AMP). If you have been a religious Christian up until now, I want to encourage you to swap out your religion and religious ideals for the truth of God's Word alone.

God's Word is Truth! The way to identify Truth is that it does not change and it does not change because it is right the first time! Traditions are fine, if they are based in Truth. Traditions are far from fine when they lead astray and block the Divine when placed above the Truth God has held firm to in His Word. Again, the emphasis must be made to throw off the old sinful nature and your former way of life, which is corrupted by lust and deception. Instead, let God's Spirit renew your thoughts and attitudes. Put on your new nature, created to be like God, truly Righteous and Holy (Ephesians 4:22-24 AMP).

Familial ties are very strong and under the law of sin and death are very binding! This is what Love does for you. It may have not been God's Design on *how* you were conceived and regardless of the circumstances of your birth, the fact that you are here is testament to God's Plan for your life. All souls come from God. We don't get here of our own accord. It is true that the natural laws of conception are in place, but the bottom line is that *only* God can spark life. With this in mind, it is by His Authorization that you are here (Jeremiah 1:5; Psalm 139:16 AMP; Ezekiel 18:4a)!

This means God has a Purpose for you! Whether steeped with good intentions or mired in motiveless malignancy, Love frees you from the traditions and pit falls of men in order for you to find that purpose! Whether you come from Alcoholics, Drug Addicts, adulterers, fornicators, incest or rape, your legacy has changed as a child of God when you choose the Path of Love! The only real disgrace with the conception of life is when that life is not laid down in service to God. This is Faith's Framework of Inheritance, powered by God's full potential to have a purpose filled, victorious and guilt free life. It is also essential to be properly framed in the understanding of why it is vital to not only accept Christ as Savior, but to also establish Him as Lord.

Chapter Seventeen

GOD'S DUAL KINGDOM

Yours, O Lord, is the greatness and the power and the glory and the victory and the majesty, indeed
everything that is in the heavens and on the earth; Yours is the dominion and kingdom, O Lord,
and You exalt Yourself as head over all. Both riches and honor come from You, and You
rule over all. In Your hand is power and might; and it is in Your hands to
make great and to give strength to everyone.
~ 1 Chronicles 29:11-13

I f you are a person who has stumbled repeatedly over the difficult and seemingly insurmountable complications of your past, I'm here to tell you that you are free in Christ! Blaming your parentage or lack thereof, your culture, your race or background for your lot in life is a wasted pursuit. These things do not matter in the lineage of Christ. As a Christian, you do live in this world, but you are not to be defined by this world nor be conformed to this world (John 17:16; Romans 12:2).

Ephesians 1:3-14 basically states, as a Child of God, you are taken to the high places of His Blessings through Christ. Long before God ever laid down earth's foundations, He had you in mind to settle the focus of His Love upon and because of this; you are made whole and Holy by His Love. Keep in mind, when you accepted Christ, God adopted you into His family! This is a very important point as I'm sure you've guessed because it's been repeated throughout this book and bears repeating once again.

Through Jesus Christ, you have entered into the celebration of your New Father's lavish gift-giving by the Hand of His Beloved Son. The Messiah's Sacrifice, His Blood being poured out on the altar of the Cross, made you a free person, free from the penalties and punishments amassed due to all your misdeeds as well as generational iniquities. You are not barely free; you are *abundantly* free!

God thought of it all and provided for everything you could possibly need. It's in Christ that you find out who you are and what your purpose is for living. Man's traditions, cultural dictates and racial conformities not only divide people, but are confining and can lead to confusion or utter chaos. These strictures will *limit* God's Plan for your life if they are opposed to His Will *for* your life. It's best to just stick with God's Plan. Only God's Way leads to a full and overflowing life. Long before you first heard of Christ, God had His eye on you and had designs on you for glorious living (Colossians 2:8; John 10:10; Jeremiah:1:5a).

Part of His overall Purpose is being worked out in everything and in everyone. The Word of God is very clear; it's in Christ that you are home free—signed, sealed, and delivered by the Holy Spirit. In Christ, you are who God says you are! Therefore, you are not defined by where you came from, nor are you constrained by those from whom you've descended. Blood tells! The Blood of Jesus overcomes any bloodline coursing through your veins. Andraé Crouch got it right back in 1970 when he wrote, *The Blood Will Never Lose Its Power* (Hebrews 9:11-28)!

Consequently, do not let Love be denied because you choose to remain bound to deals from which God's Love and Christ's Blood has freed you! This seal from God is the first installment on what's coming, a reminder that you now have access to everything God has planned for you, a praiseworthy and glorious Life here on earth and into Eternity.

This brings us once again to KINship and KINGship mentioned back in Chapter Eight and merits a more in-depth acknowledgement and understanding. Remember, Grace authorizes the expectation Hope releases for Love to flow freely and Faith is the framework through which Love is communicated. When the framework of Faith has not been established appropriately in an area of understanding, nothing of substance or stability is available to guide or sustain you on the path of Love in that area (see Chapter Nine).

Also bear in mind, the path of Love is freedom! Therefore, a framework must be established to walk in the freedom that is already yours through Christ concerning your life. Unfortunately, KINship and KINGship are concepts of which Faith's framework has been established incorrectly for many people or has never been established at all.

Kingdom of Heaven

Matthew 3:1-2 reads, *"John the Baptist, preaching in the wilderness of Judaea, and saying, Repent ye: for the Kingdom of Heaven is at hand."* The **Kingdom** here is *basileia* (bä-sē-lā'-ä) and means royal power, kingship, dominion and rule. **Heaven** is *ouranos* (ü-rä-no›s) and refers to the universe, the region above the celestial heavens, the seat of order of things eternal and consummately perfect where God and other heavenly beings dwell. John the Baptist, in these scriptures, heralds the arrival of God's Empowerment as well as the admittance to where God dwells.

The first part of your inheritance as a Believer is Kinship, your implemented bond with God through the *saving* Power of His Grace. This is yours through the repentance of your sins and the accepting of Christ's Sacrifice. By doing so, you received God's Spirit when He adopted you as His Own Child. This happened when you accepted Jesus as *SAVIOR* and, as mentioned before, is what many people flippantly refer to as fire insurance to miss hell.

God's remarkable compassion and favor drew you to Christ. God's Grace actually delivered you from judgment and has given you Eternal Life through Faith in His Son, Jesus. You did not obtain this Salvation through your own effort. Nor will Salvation be sustained by putting forth your own energy to be a good little Christian steeped in legalism or by towing the proverbial holy line on the correct side of a moral code. It is an undeserved, Gracious Gift from God; His unmerited Favor! Jesus did all the heavy lifting so to speak. All you had to do was receive it (Romans 8:15; 10:9-10; Ephesians 1:5; Galatians 4:7; Ephesians 2:8). This is straight forward. Salvation is God's free gift to all who believe on His Son Jesus Christ!

As a Believer, Heaven is now your home. You do not have to work for it! You literally have fire insurance to miss hell because you have a seat on the proverbial plane to Glory. It's in the bag—however belief unto Salvation is not the Faith that pleases God (refer back to Chapter Nine). This is where many people get confused and miss the mark of God's meaning in the area of Heaven's Eternal Reward and Grace's earthly empowerment. The Kingdom of Heaven is primarily where God dwells with Jesus seated on His Right Hand, from where God's Power originates and where we'll go when we are divested of our fleshly bodies (Mark 16:19, James 1:17, 2 Corinthians 5:8). This brings us to the second part of your inheritance, which involves the Kingdom of God.

Kingdom of God

Matthew 6:33 reads, *"But seek ye first the Kingdom of God, and His righteousness; and all these things shall be added unto you."* **Kingdom** here again is *basileia* (bä-sē-lā'-ä) and means royal power, kingship, dominion and rule. **God** is *Theos* (the-o's) and refers to the embodiment of the Trinity and whatever can in any respect be likened unto The Father, Son or Holy Spirit, or resemble God in any way. **Righteousness** is *dikaiosynē* (dē-kī-o-sü'-nā) and is the condition acceptable to God involving integrity, virtue, purity of life, correctness of thinking, feeling and acting.

In other words, you are urged to first and foremost seek, aim at and strive after the royal Power, kingship, dominion and rule of God through whatever can in any respect be likened unto or resemble God in any way. By doing so, you will attain a pure life that reveals correct thinking, positive feelings and moral actions through the attitude and character of God.

As you reach this condition acceptable to God, all your everyday human concerns will be met in full! It is KINGship or right standing with God that gives you access to the fullness of His Grace, His Empowerment. KINGship is having the graceful *empowerment* of His Unlimitless Power! The Authority to be able to lay hands on the sick so they recover; the Authority to speak to the mountains in your life and have them move; the Authority to call the intangible things into existence is within your reach (Mark 16:18b; Mark 11:23; Romans 4:17)!

This Power and Authority become accessible when you accept Jesus as LORD. There is a difference! *Accepting Jesus as Savior does not automatically make Him Lord of your life.* It is important to understand this fact. Savior and Lord are *NOT* synonymous. Jesus being your Savior is God's Gift to you. Jesus being your Lord is your Gift to God. The Amplified of Philippians 2:12b, informs you are to *work* out your own soul's salvation, to cultivate it and bring it to full effect by actively pursuing spiritual maturity using serious caution and critical self-evaluation to avoid anything that might offend God or discredit the Name of Christ. This is when you are on the road to making Jesus Lord of your life. The more you yield to the Truth of God's Word, allowing Him to saturate your heart and transform your life, the more His Power will reside within you, to operate in what frees you—Love!

Perspective

Christian Ministers in the pulpits of our churches, Missionaries in the fields of our world and televangelists broadcasting across our nation's airwaves and beyond are supposed to all have one thing in common—the Great Commission—found in Mark 16:15. This reads, *"Go into all the world and preach the gospel to all creation"* (AMP). It is the message of Salvation! It is the building block of bringing God's Kingdom to the masses! Without Salvation there is no link to a Life hid with Christ in God. It is the beginning of life's great adventure! However, The Kingdom of Heaven and The Kingdom of God make The Gospel twofold and it is the latter Kingdom that's getting lost in the Gospel's impartation.

Think of what you know about a wedding, either having experienced getting married for yourself, having attended one or having been a part of what it takes to pull one off. The investment of money, time and energy involved could be daunting. All the planning, the invitations, the long and arduous preparations involved just for that *ONE* day to be perfect and as memorable as possible! This is like Salvation. Accepting the Gift of God and receiving The Kingdom of Heaven. Like the Wedding Day, it was intended as a onetime event that opens the door to all God has for you! The genuine, long-term challenges come once all the fanfare and excitement that culminated in Salvation (the wedding) dies down and the Life hid with Christ in God (the marriage) begins.

As with marriage, the Life hid with Christ in God is muddled through based on conjecture, false expectations and uninspired advice and basically gets neglected overtime due to the disillusionment spawned by those false assumptions, bad ideologies and myth-information. Who talks about this? Think about it! It's nowhere near the hype "Getting Saved" gets. Please, don't misunderstand, Salvation is important! Just as there is no marriage without a wedding (or legal proceeding), there is no Godly Empowerment without Salvation. It starts the ball rolling! Without Salvation there is no next step.

My point is that Salvation is not the END, it is the *BEGINNING*! The door is open with repentance and accepting Christ, but without His Empowerment we will fall short in our ability to live a life of real substance—this includes our ability to Love. There is no room in Love for fear. The inheritance we received from our earthly lineage is corrupt and deeply flawed due to sin. Sin came into the world through one man, and death through sin spread to all people with no one being able to stop it or escape its power until Christ's Sacrifice. That which is born of the flesh is flesh, and that which is born of the Spirit is Spirit (Romans 5:12; John 3:6).

When you follow your flesh, you are *subject* to your earthly inheritance. When you follow God's Spirit, you are *equipped* by your God Ordained Inheritance. As God's child, you now have a *dual* inheritance.

Familial curses are your inheritance, if you yield to your flesh. The Kingship of Christ is your inheritance, if you yield to the Spirit and choose not to fulfill the lust of your flesh. The power is transferred to whichever you yield, your flesh or God's Spirit. Following God will empower the path to walk in Love. Always remember that God Himself *Is* Love (Galatians 6:8; 1 John 4:8 AMP).

When you take up permanent residence in a Life of Love, you live in God and God lives in you. This way Love has full control, becomes at home and matures in you, and frees you from worry because Love banishes fear. Fear is crippling: a fearful life, fear of death, fear of judgment. If you struggle with fear of any kind, it is an indication you are not yet fully formed in Love (1 John 4:17; 18 MSG).

The Apostle Paul urges you to press on to possess that perfection for which Christ Jesus took hold of you and made you His own. Focus on this one thing; forgetting the past and looking forward to what lies ahead, press on to reach the end of the race and receive the heavenly prize for which God, through Christ Jesus, is calling you. There are many whose conduct shows they are really enemies of the Cross of Christ. They are headed for destruction. Their god is their appetite, they brag about shameful things, and they think only about this life here on earth. As a child of God, you are a citizen of Heaven, where the Lord Jesus Christ lives. Eagerly wait for Him to return as your Savior by displaying every day that He is your Lord (Philippians 3:14-20 AMP)!

This is the KINGship of God or right standing with God which gives you access to the fullness of His Grace, His Empowerment. Do not intertwine the Kingdom of Heaven with the Kingdom of God. Although they are related, they are still mutually exclusive. Accepting Jesus as Savior invites God into your life but this does not automatically make Him Lord of your life. You must daily put Him first by seeking Him. It is a willful choice, an act of freewill.

Your *Who* determines your destination *after* this life. Your *Do* determines your destiny *in* this life. Who you are through Christ Jesus is your salvation from death (a life apart from God in Eternity). What you *do with* your life is to be identified completely with Christ because you have been essentially crucified with Him, so it is no longer you who lives, but Christ Who now lives in you. The life you now live is no longer your life, so live it by adhering to, relying on, and completely trusting in the Son of God, who Loved you so completely, He gave Himself up for you (Galatians 2:20 AMP)! Be fueled by Love. The Kingdom of God is here for you to get fully formed in Love. Since God is Love it is obvious we need more of God! How do we "get more" of Him? We must Level Up!

Chapter Eighteen

LEVEL UP

There's a way of life that looks harmless enough look again—it leads
straight to hell. Sure, those people appear to be having a good
time, but all that laughter will end in heartbreak.
~ Proverbs 14:12 (MSG)

According to the Cambridge Online Dictionary, level-up is a gaming term describing an increase in the capabilities of a character in a computer game to enable a player to go up to a higher or more difficult level, gaining more skills or strength. I am not a gamer, but from what I understand, the character icon or avatar represents the individual person playing the computer game. The more knowledge the player has about the game, coupled with the tasks and stages completed by his or her avatar, will increase the players Level of Power or accessories needed to achieve advantage and ultimate victory in the game.

Life is not a game, there is no reset button for do overs and unlike that crazy cat saying, we don't have nine lives. However, we can still Level Up with more knowledge, power and accessories needed to achieve the fruition of an Abundant Life hid with Christ in God! In an earlier chapter, we covered the fact that we are made after the Image and Likeness of God (Genesis 1:27AMP). Because of this, we have indigenous capabilities to forgive, to be kind, feel remorse, hope and even love. The problem with these glimmers of great promise, rests in the fact that because they are modeled after God, they are therefore limited without God.

The human condition has a great capacity to love with rudimentary intensity. However, without God, we can only scratch the surface of our own limited potential. This is Love's great purpose and its foundation was deliberately formulated to be built upon and expanded.

To quote the Christian Singer Carman, "If there's a design, there's a Designer, if there's a plan, there's a Planner..." You were fearfully and wonderfully made by God and the plans and thoughts that He has for you are plans for peace and well-being and not for disaster, to give you a future and a hope (Psalm 139:14; Jeremiah 29:11 AMP). Even though you came to this life through your parents, the quintessential you, your soul, came from God. You belong to Him and as a Believer you have already won a big victory, for the Spirit in you is far Stronger than anything in the world. It is also in Him that you live, move, and have your being. God dwells more deeply within you as you learn to Love (Ezekiel 18:4; 1 John 4:4, 12; Acts 17:28). The more you allow His Love to dwell in you and His Love becomes complete in you, perfect Love will result!

Okay—reality check! If you've made it this far, you are probably saying to yourself, "All of this sounds really good, but totally unrealistic! The world just doesn't work this way!" I know, I know! The kicker is that you are absolutely right! The world does *not* work this way! Unfortunately, the way the world is now is not the Eden God originally designed. The world we see now is sin riddled and iniquity saturated due to the fall of man (Romans 5:12).

People are following and are influenced by this present age in accordance with the prince of the power of the air (satan), the spirit who is now at work in the disobedient and the unbelieving, the very one who actively fights against the Purposes of God. This pursuance is why this world is interwoven with the evil of the enemy, but God wants to interweave your world with the beauty of His Grace. It is true we live *in* this world, but we are not to be conformed *to* this world (Ephesians 2:2; Romans 12:2). It is in no way a hidden secret how challenging the mission to choose to Love can be when the people you Love elect to be unaccommodating at best and totally pugnacious at their worst!

This is the crux of the problem. Basing our willingness to Love on the actions of others is the same as being unable to see the forest because of all those annoying trees. If you are seeking to apply it in your own strength, the battle is already lost! It is also true, due to choices imposed upon us by others in authority over us, or our own choices made out of ignorance or rebellion, our lives do not fit into a nice, neat bow of God's expected Standards as detailed in the previous chapters.

The framework laid out for us in God's Word is what God *intended* for humanity to follow from inception. The radical way in which your life may differ from His Original Plan became totally irrelevant when you accepted His Son. His Ultimate Destiny designed for your Life is still yours and is waiting for you to make up your mind to hold fast to *His* Plan. Let go of what is now behind you and what others tell you is best for you and focus on the goal, where God is beckoning you onward—to Jesus. So, get to stepping! In fact, sprint in that direction and do not think about turning back (Philippians 3:14 MSG)!

We are bombarded constantly with information contrary to God and His Word. These deceptions are presented in ways that pull on the heart strings or incite our spirit of adventure! You may say, "C'mon! It's just entertainment!" It's far from *just* entertainment! It is a stratum of programing so refined and invasive that the masses, somewhere along the line, have missed the subtle turning of their cautionary switches to off!

The fact that our original design was based on Who God Is means we have an internal switch for moral living. The problem with Believers comes in when we don't know God's Word. God freely gives out Wisdom, and from His Word comes knowledge and understanding. He stores away sound wisdom for you when you are in right standing with Him. He is a Shield to you when you walk in honorable character and moral courage. He guards the paths of justice and preserves your way as one of His Believers, so Level Up by studying God's Word which by design, will sanction your heart to keep His commandments (Hosea 4:6; Proverbs 2:6-8 AMP; James 1:5; Psalm 31:23).

The words found within the Bible's pages will help you live a long life: whole, full of blessings—a life worth living. In His Word resides Wisdom which encompasses prudence, good judgment, moral courage, astute common sense, and it seeks out knowledge and discretion. The acceptance of God's Word brings a Leveling Up of all these accessories to moral character as well as reverential fear and worshipful awe of the Lord (Proverbs 8:10-12 AMP).

This in turn produces an abhorrence of evil, a turning away of pride, arrogance and the desire to put away evil ways along with perverted conversation. Counsel is found in God's Word. Sound wisdom, understanding, power and strength are yours when you do not forget His teaching. By doing so, you'll do your best to present yourself to God approved, a laborer, tested by trial with no reason to be ashamed because you are accurately handling and skillfully teaching the Word of Truth in the everyday living of your life (Proverbs 8:13,14 AMP; 2 Timothy 2:15).

When you choose to Level Up, mercy, kindness and truth will be qualities that define you. So, metaphorically bind God's Words securely around your neck and figuratively write them on the tablet of your heart. By doing so, you'll earn a reputation for living well in God's Eyes and the eyes of the people with whom you interact every day (Proverbs 3:1-4 AMP). Again, if anyone tells you otherwise, I can *guarantee,* they are trying to sell you something!

This is real warfare for your body, your soul and your spirit! Believe it! All the ungodly, immoral ideas hitting you are brash, discouraging, relentless and licentious, because the world is unprincipled and ruled by an enemy determined to destroy you any way he can. It's ruthless out there! The world hits below the belt. Be assured, we as God's children, do not live or fight our battles the way the world does—never have and never will if we want victory (2 Corinthians 10:3 MSG).

The tools of our trade aren't for promotion or manipulation, but they are for demolishing the entire massively corrupt culture all around us. We are to use our powerful, divinely honed implements for smashing warped philosophies, tearing down barriers erected against the Truth of God, fitting every loose thought and emotion and impulse into the structure of a life shaped by Christ. Our Spiritually empowered devices are ready and at hand for clearing the ground of every obstruction and building lives of obedience into the maturity found only through honoring God's

Directives, instead our own rules—limited by finite understanding (2 Corinthians 10:4-6 MSG).

Have you been saved for a time? Test yourself to make sure you are solid in the Faith. Don't just drift along taking everything for granted. Give yourself a checkup. You need firsthand evidence, not mere hearsay that Jesus Christ is in you. Test it out. Do you take your everyday, ordinary life: your sleeping, eating, going-to-work, and walking-around life, and place it before God as an offering daily? If you fail the test, do something about it (2 Corinthians 13:5; Romans 12:1 MSG)!

Are you a New Believer? You must learn the Way of the Lord. You must find that Life hid with Christ in God. It is a new way of learning to do old things: a new walk, a new talk and a new way. It's not an outward show, but an inward change which will reveal itself in an outward expression (Colossians 3:3; 2 Corinthians 5:17).

I'm not talking about an overnight over hall like Toby McGuire's Peter Parker experienced after that infamous spider bite, where he went from scrawny, pencil-thin weakling to a web-slinging, acrobatic, chiseled Hero the next day. Nor is there an intimation that you must throw out all of your secular CD's to replace them with extemporaneous, classically charged refrains!

I am talking about living your life sculpted through the framework of Faith, infused by Love. The Fear, Uncertainty and Doubt (FUD) Campaign reigns supreme in this world because it plays to human greed, manipulates strong emotions and flows nicely with the devil's plan to reap as many souls as possible in order to deny God His Children's Love. Living life the world's way is to live life steeped in fear. Fear of not having enough. Fear of losing what you do have. Fear of illness. Fear of death. Fear of harm. Fear of failure. Fear of fear itself! The list is endless! This way may seem the correct way because it's reflected in the way most of the populist live their lives; even more so because many Christian leaders unfortunately live their lives this way as well. However, just because the majority may follow a way that seems right, that way is not always correct just because the majority believes it to be truth (Proverbs 14:2).

If you find you share this way with the masses, think of *who* sold you the idea, but don't dwell on when and where you bought it, or even when you decided to bring it home to take up residence in your soul, instead realize where this way is leading your life. If the direction is leading you away from the Way that God has planned in His Word, put on the brakes! Take a hint from Mark Twain, "Whenever you find yourself on the side of the majority, it is time to pause and reflect." I like to add in regard to secular understanding, "and generally go in the *opposite* direction" which nine out of ten times, turns out to be God's Way anyway!

You are to follow only God, hold *Him* in deep admiration, keep *His* commandments and listen obediently to what *He* says, serve *Him* and hold onto *Him* for dear life. Don't become so well-adjusted to your culture or societal agenda that you fit into it without even thinking. Instead, live on purpose! Fix your attention on God. You'll be changed from the inside out. Readily recognize what He wants from you, and quickly respond to it. Unlike the social dictates around you, always dragging you down to its level of immaturity, God will bring out the best in you and will develop a well-formed maturity in you (Deuteronomy 13:4; Romans 12:2MSG)!

It is God and *only* God Who can equip you with a wise mind and a spirit, attuned to achieving what you were designed to achieve, as you acquire a strong framework of Faith through understanding the ways in which He works. As you increasingly learn how God operates in all things through the studying of His Word and communing with Him in prayer, you will gain a deeper Faith, clearer insight and fervent Joy only His precepts and enlightenment can awaken.

You'll have the strength to outlast whatever trials you face with the knowledge that as hardships and perplexing circumstances confront you, it is the Lord Who rescues you from them all as you trust and rely on Him (Psalm 34:19). Not a contrived strength, through gritting your teeth in tolerance in an effort to manufacture happiness, but the glorious strength to let go of what you cannot change, gravitate to what you can and have the insight to know the difference between the two.

It is strength, remunerated and exemplified by Leveling Up in Love, which will cause you to not be struck dumb with utter amazement, be surprised or enraged when you go through ordeals calculated to test the quality of your Faith. You won't react as though something strange or unusual is happening to you, but will instead act upon God's Word in Faith, knowing God is on the job to make the way of escape or to provide the wherewithal to stand and endure to the end. You will thank God as He makes you strong enough to take part in everything bright and beautiful that He has for you after you've accepted His Salvation (Colossians 1:9-12 MSG).

God rescued you from the dead-end alleyways and the dark dungeons of sin's torment. He's set you up in the Kingdom of His dear Son, the Son who got you out of the pit you were in by getting rid of the power the sins you were doomed to keep repeating, had over you (Colossians 1:13,14 MSG; 1 Peter 4:12, 13). Remember— you are FREE! So, let go of the fear found in *failing* to Love. Embrace the Joy of God's Eternal Redemption and receive all of Him by *choosing* to Love!!!

In Him there is Peace, Joy, the freedom to Love and where Hope abides! Hope does not put you to shame, because God's Love has been poured into your heart through the Holy Spirit (Romans 5:5). God didn't go through all this trouble to leave you to your own devices! With this in mind, it is your responsibility to seek Him for His Purpose for your life and to Level Up in Love. I'm not telling you something someone told me. I'm not passing on some idealistic doctrine I picked up along the way because I go to church. I'm telling you what I know to be true because I live it every day! As Mahalia Jackson sang it best: *My God is Real*—not only because I can feel Him in my soul, but because of His evident Presence in my life!

My Testimony

I married a saved, sanctified, Holy Ghost filled Man of God with vision and a heart to do God's Will. However, after having married on one accord with a laid-out Vision from God for our lives, two children and twenty-one years of marriage, the man I Love decided he no longer wanted to be married to me! With no warning, preemptive strikes, rhyme, reason or explanation, he filed for divorce and meant it.

As a very active parent, attentive to my children's education and school functions, I spent numerous hours volunteering at their schools throughout the years and this day was no different than any other. I'd returned home after selling ice cream to raise money for the Band, an activity I oversaw as Band Treasurer. Soon after changing my outside clothes to more comfortable home attire, the doorbell rang. In the process of descending the stairs from the upper level to answer the front door, I called out, "You expecting something?" thinking a package of his was being delivered. There was no response. Upon opening the door, I was confronted with a Sherriff's Deputy serving me with Divorce papers! I kid you not, I actually leaned out of the door to spot the candid cameras because I just *knew* I was being punked!

After closing the door, I turned around to see him standing there so I asked in disbelief, "Is this for real?" He replied in the affirmative. I then asked, "Can we talk about this?"

He sternly said "No!" turned his back on me and walked away.

I went back upstairs on autopilot. Autopilot meaning the punched drunk, head spinning turmoil I could imagine a boxer feels going down after a swift one-two punch right before his head bounces off the weathered floor of the well-used ring! Dazed and confused doesn't even come close to describing it! However, I was *still* rooted in Christ (Matthew 7:24-25)! The flesh wanted to rage, but God's Spirit engaged and kept me calm, reasonable and trusting in His Will to prevail.

When you allow God to rule, your default position will change from reactive to trusting. I immediately prayed and sought God's Direction in the situation. At this point, Jesus had been Lord of my life for 28 years! True worship, real service and a yielded life gave way to a strength that surpassed all understanding. Was I in emotional turmoil? Yes! Did I allow this to deter my ability to choose God's way? No!

You see, Elnora's daughter wanted to go all Army on his behind, pop a cap and break some bones, but God's Child rose up in me and LOVE prevailed so that peace could manifest and God's Favor could flow, allowing my heart and mind to remain open to Him. He gave me direction and my heart did not faint because changing circumstances do not negate God's Ability to move as His Word Promises when you choose to believe Him and not your circumstances. Love chose to believe God.

I wanted my husband to come to his senses so we could work things out. Love is blind to negative stimuli and looks for a positive outcome, so I prayed and believed God for my marriage to be restored. Even though my husband was willing to do so, the investment of nearly twenty-two years was not something I was willing to just throw away! However, when the unction to go to an established shelter program in my county to get a restraining order against him came upon me and the hurt and bewildered *feelings* of my flesh told me to wait until I found an attorney so he or she could sort out such things, God's *Spirit* rose up within me to get it done that day.

I'm glad I was obedient because, unbeknownst to me, my husband had filed an erroneous restraining order against me earlier that same day. Evidently, due to having a lawyer present before the Judge, his order was signed before my order was seen. Fortunately, once the Judge saw my order he called for a hearing three days later. In the interim, because my husband's order went through first, I was removed from my home under police escort at nearly midnight that night.

The flesh wanted to rage at the unfairness of the situation and cry out in anger at why God would allow this. How was this just! The Holy Spirit rose up and caused me to rest in the Word which boldly proclaims, *"Many hardships and perplexing circumstances confront the righteous, but the Lord rescues him from them all"* (Psalm 34:19 AMP).

Had I allowed my hurt feelings to rule and not been obedient to the Holy Spirit, the original signed order would have had me put out of my home for nearly twenty-eight days before seeing a judge, instead of three. When the judge realized the two complaints mirrored each other, he called for a hearing as soon as possible! Walking in the Spirit (open to God) and not yielding to my flesh (feelings) afforded me the clarity to do what made no sense to me at the time. God knew, and He made the way.

There were other vicious and cruel avenues in which the enemy used my husband to inflict confusion, emotional, mental and economic harm throughout the divorce proceedings, but God opened doors for me and my children each and every step of the way! When we had no place to go, God touched the hearts of His people to provide shelter for us. When my husband blocked the initial order for financial support during the proceedings—God made a way.

My husband was the sole support for our household, so when he refused reasonable requests like alimony and help with our children's college tuitions, the flesh wanted to fight for what was rightfully due me and our children, but Faith rose up and God spoke plainly in my spirit, "LaShanda, will you fight man for what he *might* give you, or will you believe me for what I've already promised you?"

'Nuf said! My spirit agreed with God and said, "Lord, have your way!"

A failure to Love follows the world's advice and says, "Take him for all he's worth because he owes you!"

God says, "Trust me, I'll make a way because I've already paid it all!"

God never said His Way would be easy, but He did Promise it would be worth it (Galatians 6:9)! It is true everyone's state of affairs is different. Another person in my situation may have had to go a different route than the one God led me. This is where that Life hid with Christ in God comes in. He will lead and guide you. He did this for me and I can say because He did, I made it through— by His Grace, I endured!

Things did not go the way I wanted—bright rays of sunlight didn't break boldly through the clouds, harps didn't play, fat little baby cherubs didn't sing and my husband did not "see the light" nor change his course—so three days after our twenty-second wedding anniversary, I was a divorced woman!

There I was, divorced, homeless, without any financial support for me, nor for our children's educations, with one child in college and another just graduated from High School—on the way to college. I had no job, no money and no prospects! The future, the life I thought was mine—gone! A pile of ashes on the altar of broken promises and unfulfilled dreams. The flesh says, "You are worthless and unloved so be ashamed, crawl into the deepest part of yourself and die!"

The Spirit countered with, "Jesus is in the Presence of The Father at this very moment sticking up for you. Do you think anyone is going to be able to drive a wedge between you and Christ's Love for you? There is no way! Not a divorce, not hard times, not hatred, not hunger, not homelessness, not bullying threats, not backstabbing! Let none of this faze you because Jesus Loves you. Be absolutely convinced that nothing: nothing living or dead, angelic or demonic, today or tomorrow, high or low, thinkable or unthinkable, absolutely *nothing* can get between you and God's Love for you! You matter, you are precious and you are honored because you are Loved by God (Romans 8:38,39; Isaiah 43:4a)!"

If you didn't already know, I can assure you that anger has a voice and it will speak loud and determinately when unsolicited and unwanted, especially when fueled by offence. Anger sat down with me one day and told me to forget about Love because it wasted my youth and gave me only what turned out to be false promises and a misused life. Anger insisted I blame and accuse. After all, I spent decades Loving a man who "threw me away" for no reality based reason and without rational explanation.

Love rose up, chased away blame and reminded me it was *man's* failure to Love and *not* Love who gave me false promises. It was man's choice to depart, making *his* promises null and void. It is *God* Who Promises to restore. I am a tither and a giver and had been at that point, all the then twenty-eight years that Jesus was Lord of my life, so he caused people to be a blessing to me. Government assistance was not needed. *God* made all Grace, every favor and earthly blessing come in abundance to me, so that I under all circumstances, regardless of the need, had complete sufficiency in everything, being completely self-sufficient in Him, and I had an abundance for every good work and act of charity. The Love of fellow Believers and the kindness of strangers can be humbling in the abundance of its expression (2 Corinthians 9:8; Luke 6:38 AMP).

I've even had one of the many people who God has used to be a blessing to me and my children ask, "Why you? Out of all the many people I could bless, why you?" The only thing I can say is that it has very little to do with me personally, a lot to do with obedience and everything to do with the faithfulness of my God!

You can never rise if you never have anything to rise above! Leveling up is not just a gaming construct! It can outline a way of life designed by God to support and sustain a Life of Power, Peace and Privilege. The framework of Faith is a leveling up strategy! Faith, piled up and stored, is useless without it being tested and tried. Therefore, it is the tougher more challenging road that makes us capable of achieving things we never thought we could. The harder journey, when given to God, leads to a greater purpose and a richer destiny.

I got a job, a place to live and while I was well below the poverty line, I was able to pay my rent on time, eat and get the supplies needed to live comfortably. The flesh would want to complain about what I lost, but God's Spirit rose up in me and gratefulness permeated my soul and praise filled the halls of my heart at the peace I gained. God gave me favor on that job and after a year, opened an unexpected door for a better more sustaining job with people who are a joy to work with and benefits that made me weep because they are such an exceptional blessing.

At the writing of these pages, my daughter has gotten her bachelor's degree and is working on her master's degree, my son's on the Dean's List and will be working on his Senior year in college this fall! All without the help of the man the enemy tried to use to sift us like wheat. God is making a way at every turn! We are doing well and have hope for a bright and prosperous future! As the song says, "My God is Awesome! He can move mountains! Keeps me in the valley and hides me from the rain!" The world's impossible becomes God's Possible when we rely on Him and when we believe Him and are obedient to what He asks!

Every room has an entry and every lock has a key. God's key is CHOICE. If it seems evil or unreasonable to serve the Lord, then don't serve Him, but *choose* whom you *will* serve! Do not let your loyalty be divided between God and the world! If you do this, you will be unstable in everything you do. (Joshua 24:15; James 1:8). Going to church on Sunday, Bible Study on Wednesday and Friday Night Praise Service is great, but if God is only God when you are there, you are again missing the forest because of all those pesky trees! God is God ALL THE TIME!

Faith's framework of leveling up requires an all-in mentality. Even though my life is *far* from perfect, God moved miraculously for me because He is not my God *just* during those miniscule hours I go to church. He is my God twenty-four-seven! He wants all of you and is willing to give all to you! He started with giving you life and is all-in by saving that life through the sacrifice of His Son. So will you rise to the challenge of being all-in as well?

Chapter Nineteen

ALL IN

Throw off your old sinful nature and your former way of life, which is
corrupted by lust and deception. Instead, let the Spirit renew your
thoughts and attitudes. Put on your new nature, created
to be like God—truly righteous and holy
~ Ephesians 4:22-24 (NLT)

When I was in the military I was initiated through a process called Basic Training. I didn't join the Army one day and the next day get placed on the front lines in a war. I was inducted through an eight-week block of instruction on how the military worked, what was expected and how I was to conduct and defend myself and my country as a soldier of the United States Army. Basic was then followed by Military Occupation Specialties Training in my chosen field. Once MOS training was completed, I was shipped to my permanent duty station where I continued to receive periodic training session as well as being expected to meet physical training requirements once a month.

I was property of the US Government. I ate, slept and breathed the military! The Army was responsible for my housing, clothing, food and livelihood. There were rules and detailed accountabilities, spoken and unspoken expectations. It was life twenty-four-seven and it was real! I couldn't decide today I was not going to work. I couldn't decide the orders I would follow from the ones I deemed unnecessary. I couldn't leave of my own volition. Under the Uniform Code of Military Justice, I would have been considered AWOL or Absent without Leave. This would have resulted in Court Martial—a judicial court for trying members of the Armed

Services accused of offenses against military law. I had account-ability and I was held to that accountability every second of every minute, every minute of every hour, every hour of every day, every day of every year I served.

I was not actively conscience of this accountability every second. However, if a violation occurred, I would have been swiftly reminded! Being in the military was not an addition *to* my life. In an inherent sense, the military *was* my life. The military is a natural entity. It's made up and run by fallible individuals. It's imperfect and its objectives at times could even be immoral. However, this entity, for a time, had total control over my very existence.

You may not have served in a branch of the Armed Forces, but you may have a job or a task of accountably with adherable param-eters. It may not be as invasive or all-encompassing as military ser-vice, but has consequences of some kind if violations occur. The point is, you humble yourself in response to your need to eat, have a roof over your head, drive a cool ride or have the freedom to raid the next sale at Macy's or Ben Sherman. You do what's necessary to produce a lifestyle or standard of living you want or strive to obtain. This is a basic need for survival as well as a bent toward wish fulfillment and vice.

The authorities to which you yield are mere mortals, just as you are. You go where they tell you and do what they've tasked you with, knowing if you don't, you'll eventually suffer the con-sequences. You may or may not get the recognition or the proper pay for your service, yet you do what you must do to survive. This is my point. Be honest with yourself, do you give service to the people who demand your time, energy and effort in return for com-paratively little compensation and give very little if any real service the God of the Universe, who gives you the very air you breathe and has set into motion the principles that allow your heart to beat, without your conscious effort?

Do you show difference or pay real homage to The One Who has given you great and precious promises of inexpressible value? God's Promises afford you the opportunity to escape from the immoral abandon that is in the world because of disreputable desires and enable you to share His Divine Nature. Most importantly, HE

IS THE *ONLY* ONE WHO CAN *ACTUALLY* DELIVER ALL OF WHAT HE HAS PROMISSED YOU (2 Peter 1:4; 2 Corinthians 1:20 AMP)!

As a Believer, who has been in Christ for a while but have not had your mind renewed, this is a wakeup call! As a new Believer, one recently saved, this is your call to arms!!! Remember, everyone who belongs to Christ has become a new person. The old life is gone! A new life has begun, so act like it! Like when I was in the military, the military *was* the life—in Christ, your life is *His Life*! He purchased you with the shed Blood of His Son. Your life is now His. He did not buy you as a slave to do His bidding. He instead purchased your freedom from sin into His Everlasting Life and the fullness of His Grace. He is not an addition to life, but *Is* Life itself (Romans 5:9; John 1:4).

God is not an accessory you adorn on Sunday morning before you go to church like gold cufflinks or a wide brimmed hat. He is EVERYTHING! This makes Love EVERYTHING! We covered in Chapter Four how perception is nine-tenths of a Life. View God as He is. As His Word, the Bible says He Is. Not how society, Grandma's religion or people whose worship is a farce and teach man-made ideas as if they are commands from God, says He Is (Mark 7:7).

The old man is dead, so throw off the trappings of the old sinful nature wrapped up in your former way of thinking, which is corrupted by lust and deception. Instead, let God's Spirit renew your thoughts and attitudes. Put on your New Nature, created to be like God—truly Righteous and Holy (Ephesians 4:22-24). It will not just happen! You must seek God for His Empowerment. Then and only then will you be able to Love as God Loves. Your natural love is not enough. It is fueled by your own efforts and emotions and therefore will fail, unable to stand the test of time.

You are a creature whose greatest fuel source is Love. This is how God designed you. Consider the Food Processor by Cuisinart as an example of design and purpose. Cuisinart, according to Cuisinart.com, is an American home appliance brand owned by The Conair Corporation. The company was started in 1971 by Carl Sontheimer to bring an electric food processor to the US market.

The "Food Processor" was the first model, introduced at the National Housewares Exposition in Chicago in 1973 and released in Canada in 1975.

The Cuisinart Elemental 13 Cup Food Processor is designed to perform any food prep task your recipe calls for. Big enough to chop ingredients for a party-sized portion of salsa, the Elemental 13 can also dice ingredients in the same bowl. There are fifty-three recipes listed on the website attributed to the abilities of this well-designed machine and cookbooks dedicated to hundreds of other recipes from other sources. This versatile machine is designed to perform several tasks with varying degrees of difficulty. I'm sure with the imagination of chefs worldwide, its uses are limitless. There is only one issue with this marvelous machine—it needs a power source!

Without plugging this grand invention into a power source, regardless of any add-on attachments, it's rendered to being nothing more than an expensive paper weight! This is how you are limited when you are not plugged into The Source. You have great and latent possibilities and the means to live up to that potential, however, if you don't plug into Love, you are rendered to being only a paperweight, or doorstop maybe, in the Kingdom of God. There's nothing wrong with being a doorstop, if this was what you were designed for, but you are a top of the line Cuisinart so plug in and get to processing!

Plugging In

How do you know you're all in? When your situation starts talking to you and you start talking to your situation about your God. How do you know you're all in? When your default position has moved from fear to Faith. Fear is a tormentor; Faith is a companion. How do you know you're all in? God will supply all that you need. Through Him you have all sufficiency, when you choose the way of the Word instead of the way of the world. By doing so, you are choosing God and are choosing to Level Up and Pug In (1 John 4:18; Philippians 4:19)!

Reading the Word and receiving the Word are two different things. We can study the Word and get knowledge from the Word or we can commune with God through His Word and obtain revelation from Him as well as receive the Promises only He can redeem (2 Corinthians 9:8-13 AMP).

There is a misnomer that Love can die. If God is Love, how is this possible? As a popular movie franchise proudly proclaims: *God's Not Dead!* Therefore, neither is Love! Your love has limits and when it is reached and runs out, this is where God—Who is Love—goes on. It's also been said Love goes hot and then cold. Well again, God is Love and He baptizes with the Holy Ghost and with fire (Luke 3:16)! Last time I checked; fire was hot *not* cold!

No, Love is neither dead, dying nor cold! Love has levels. If you bottom out of your own ability to love, you are limited and will eventually fail. If you fill your Love tank through the framework of Faith, the level of Love will rise to occupy the defined spaces. Everyone unplugged bears limited fruit, but those plugged in will continue to bear fruit. God will repeatedly supply the Power, infusing you with *His* Strength so that you will bear even richer and finer fruit (John 15).

When I came to the realization that my husband had chosen to no longer Love me, we had been married for about twelve years. This realization was personified full force for me one day when the children and I were getting ready to attend church. It'd become obvious my husband had decided to turn his back on God a few years earlier and in so doing, he had become withdrawn, evil hearted and petulant! He refused to go to church, pray or have anything to do with the things of God. Consequently, on this particular Sunday morning as usual, he was not getting ready as our children and I were, to go to church and with nothing else constructive to do, he decided to harass me for some made up reason I cannot even recall.

Now don't get me wrong. My husband was a wonderful man (I would not have married him otherwise!), but I came to realize the wonderfulness of him was a direct result of his relationship with God! He was loving, attentive, resourceful in his pursuit of me and tender in his regards toward me. God Loved me *through* him. It was beyond measure how pleasing and loving my husband was toward me! We complemented and blended together in every way.

One of his sisters even commented on how changed for the better her brother was from the one she knew growing up and tried to attribute this change in him to my influence. I quickly disabused her of this assumption, stating he was already this "new way" when I met him. This change she saw in her brother is what yielding to Christ can do for a life, just as irrational behavior is what turning away from Him can do to a soul.

Well, this day it became glaringly clear I was no longer dealing with the New Man, but the old one, no longer dead in Christ but alive and in all the technicolor brilliance only the flesh can display! He was overwhelmingly vicious in his unwarranted verbal attack toward me and quite frankly (excuse my "French"), pissed—me— off! When people use the language and syntax he used toward me that day, they should no longer have any contact with each other let alone be married to one another! I made up my mind that day to rectify the *sitchiation*!

No man would talk to me that way and still have any access to me! I'm a child of God after all! A King's kid! I said not one word to him as I calmly gathered my Bible, our children and headed to church! I fumed and sputtered in my mind on how *DARE* he talk to me like this! It is *OVER*. I'm *DONE*! I don't have to take this! The world says, "Kick him to the curb girl! There are more fish in the sea!" and I agreed! Well, not about the more fish in the sea part! I was so upset at the time that *all* men could go to Hades at that point! I was beyond angry—I did not even remember the drive! I remembered the anger! The hurt! The humiliation and the determination to find a Divorce Lawyer on Monday! *IT—WAS—OVER!*

This mantra, "It's Over!" repetitively played in my head from the time the venomous words spewed from my husband's lips to the time I walked into the church building! Even though I was upset, God's Spirit still reigned Supreme. I had given God my life years ago. Yes, I was pissed, *but* I was still leveled up and all in! I was yielded, so even in anger God was able to break through a fleshly disposition to reach my heart.

Remember the mantra, playing over and over in my head? It's over? I kid you not, my children and I rounded the corner from the vestibule to face the sanctuary and upon the ushers opening the sanctuary doors, the worship leader proclaimed in a bold, clear and Spirit filled voice, "It ain't over until God says it's over. It ain't over until God says it's done. No, no, no, no, no, it ain't over until God says it's over. Keep fighting until your victory is won!" a song from the late Rev. James Moore. I was floored! The wind of discontent went out of the sails of righteous indignation and was replaced by a wind of change. I heard the still small voice of God tell me, "LaShanda, My Grace is sufficient!" I had a new lease on life because I was able to *accept* the fact my husband no longer Loved me! I was also able to understand, without his yielding to God, he was *incapable* of Loving me!

Without God we can do nothing that only His Ability can Empower us to do! I remembered my life is not my own and God made it abundantly clear that He did not want me to kick my husband to the curb by reminding me of the availability of His Grace and I have to agree—God's Grace *is* sufficient! I realized I was putting pressure on a man to do what only God could do. My husband's refusal to yield to God produced a barrier, blocking God's Ability to Empower Love's advance! This divine epiphany helped me on that day to give my husband over to God completely! I cannot express to you what God began to do for me the day I did.

The natural mind says you are wasting your time, and your life, staying with a man who obviously does not Love you. This is crazy! But God's Grace Empowered me to a Peace that surpassed all ordinary understanding! I had a renewed Joy and an ability to grow despite the restricted soil I was planted in and to Love in the midst of being unloved! Mark 10:9 of the Amplified reads, *"Therefore, what God has united and joined together, man must not separate by divorce."* This is not just a way to wax poetic, God meant what He said. So it was not within my authority to call it quits. He did not however mean for us to stay married out of some misplaced duty, but because family matters and Love is a Shield!

The framework of family detailed in Chapter Ten highlights the stabilizing factor a Family plays in our social foundation. It is not something to be thrown away because of a refusal to Love, steeped in bad feelings or discontentment. This is the ultimate in Grace's sufficiency! God can heal *your* bad feelings and discontentment by helping *you* forgive as well as face *your* own choices. A less than perfect marriage is not a misfortune, but an opportunity for growth (1 Timothy 3:5; 1 Timothy 5:8).

Fighting for Family is God's imperative. It's *His* strategy for us to have fervent and unfailing Love for one another, to overlook unkindness and selflessly seek the best for those we Love. Family is to be hospitable to one another without complaint. Each one of us as Believers, has received an ability, graciously given by God to serve one another as good stewards of God's Grace. We are to faithfully use theses varied and diverse gifts and abilities instead of nurturing anger, harboring resentment or cultivating bitterness so that grudges do not fuel us to poison or run away from the haven Family was meant to provide. To forget promises and abandon Family is giving place to the devil. It is the coward's machination toward selfish ambition (1 Peter 4:8-10 AMP; Galatians 5:22-23 MSG; Ephesians 4:27 AMP).

Spock and Captain Kirk were correct in *The Wrath of Khan* when Spock stated, "The needs of the many outweigh the needs of the few." Kirk then clarifies, "Or the one!" The choice for Family is to outweigh any personal demand that does not line up with God's Word. Giving up on Family flies in the face of Philippians 4:13 in the Amplified which states, *"[You] can do all things which [God] has called [you] to do through [Christ] who strengthens and empowers [you] to fulfill His purpose...[He will] infuse [you] with inner strength and confident peace."* Feelings whine about right now! Faith, which is fueled by Love, stands tall and chooses God's Way in defiance of circumstances (Malachi 2:13-15 MSG)!

Love allows the freedom of choice. This cannot be stressed enough! It is not about feelings! It is about allowing God's Grace to be sufficient. Because I stayed, I was able to raise my children in the fear and admonition of the Lord. No one had to tell me their first word or when they took their first step. I witnessed every season of my children's childhood. I encouraged at every pitfall and rejoiced at every triumph—firsthand! I had a front row seat to it all. The Amplified of Psalms 37:4 reads, *"Delight yourself in the LORD, and He will give you the desires and petitions of your heart."* Because I stayed, I did not miss one milestone in my children's lives and we have real relationship. We have *real* conversation. This may not be important to some, but for me—it's *priceless*!

In staying and trusting God, He can empower you to be the best *you* in the situation and to bring about the best results for *your* life and the lives *your* life touches. The charge of marriage, the charge of Family is not to be loved, but to Love. This is foundational! It is an edict from God not for duty, but for destiny (Ephesians 5:25; Ephesians 6:1-3 all AMP). God empowered me to this call so I was able to Love the unlovable and not loose who, or Whose, I was in the process.

God knew even then my husband's heart. He Knew how my husband would later allow the enemy to deceive him into discarding the family who Loves him, therefore God Empowered me in advance by fortifying my Love tank with more of Himself. When those divorce papers were in my hand, yes I was dazed, but I *couldn't* fall apart. God was upholding me with His Love! Imagine what could have happened if I had not allowed God's Grace to be sufficient, but instead chose to become bitter, resentful and vicious. Those tenants of human reasoning and weapons of false protection could have been used to utterly destroy me and set me up for an acrimonious battle against God's Way and also usher in a way for the enemy to steal my hope, kill my faith and destroy my willingness to Love.

Instead, God's Grace fortified Faith, restored Hope and upheld Love and I made it through. I have to tell you, the other side of through is much better than the place I was before. God's Grace is sufficient! You may be thinking, "If God is so Powerful, why didn't he change your husband's heart toward you, and change his mind about the divorce?" That's a good question! Let us refer back to Chapter Six.

As we have to accept another person's free will, God also respects free will. My ex-husband unplugged somewhere along the way, causing him to make that choice against God and God did not override his will. His not being connected to The Source caused him to dishonor God by refusing to rejoice in the wife of his youth. His failure to Love caused him to instead, discard the wife of his youth (Hebrews 6:4-6 MSG; Proverbs 5:18 AMP).

We, as Believers, must never fall into the mindset of spell casting when we set on a course to pray for someone. If the one to whom you are married elects to break their vows and deny Legacy through divorce, or if anyone you Love chooses a way outside of God's Will; this does not negate your vow or willingness to honor God by continuing to Love. Your prayers for an individual will open an avenue in which God can work. However, the free will of that individual will supersede any prayer, no matter how fervent or override any intervention, no matter how Divine.

Fervent prayer, on the other hand, will open an avenue in which God can transform *your* mind and subsequently *your* actions *concerning* the individual, causing the situation to line up with the Will of God in regard to *you* in the midst of the situation. Your willingness to trust Him will bring about a God-filled result, if not an outright favorable outcome for you. Even though you may not *feel* it is very favorable at the time. God uses the *willing* vessel. He does not usurp the will of the one not willing to line up with His Word. The beauty of being in right standing with God is that what the enemy means for evil, God will turn around for the good of the one who Loves and is divinely appointed by Him (James 5:16; Ecclesiastes 5:4 NLT; Romans 8:28; 2 Timothy 2:21; Genesis 50:20).

It seems as if I was discarded, but the reality of the situation is that God released us from tyranny and in turn freed me and my children for blessings too enumerable to count! Without free will, we cannot have choice. Without choice, we cannot have Love so God will not override your will or the will of others for whom you have prayed. To do so would make God disingenuous and that He is not—for the gifts and the calling of God are irrevocable. He does not withdraw what He has given. He gave us free will and will not go against His Own Word to take it back. Neither will He force His Way. He will stand at the door and knock and will patiently await entry (Romans 11:29; Revelation 3:20).

Will you allow Him entry? You are already made free by accepting Christ Who died for your sins. Level Up and get plugged into Him, so He can make you completely whole by fortifying you with more of Himself as you seek Him. Just as the Cuisinart cannot do what it was created for without being plugged into a power source, neither can you bear the fruit of Love, producing evidence of framed Faith, unless you remain plugged into God. He Is the Vine and we are the branches. The ones who remain in Him will bear much fruit. Apart from God, cut off from a vital union with Him through His Son Jesus Christ, you can do nothing that has any eternal weight in Glory. Unplugged you will eventually wither and die (John 15).

You will run out of your own ability. For instance, relationships once joyous and fulfilling will become tedious and mundane. If you remain plugged into Love without doubting God's Love for you, keep His commandments and obey His teachings, not in perfection but steady resolve, as you press toward the mark, you will remain in His Love. As you give every part of your life, everything you Love and all of who you are over to Him, He will make straight your paths. This is your Savior's Promise to you, so that His Joy and Delight may be in you, and that your joy may be made full, complete and overflowing (Philippians 3:14; John 15:10,11; Proverbs 3:6 AMP).

The ultimate in life is to plug into God and remain. The more of Him you receive, the more your Love level will rise. This is Love! It is a Cornerstone. It is perpetual. It is solid and it is everlasting! Like a magnifying glass upon the infinite stretch of our vast, ever expanding universe, Love exposes, refines and pinpoints destination. It clarifies and expands imagination. Love *IS* the singular point pertaining to all life on every level!

The bigger and more abundant the application of Love to your life, the more far reaching the ripples of Its change! As Paul encouraged the Philippian Church, I also encourage you to be well on your way and forever reach out for Christ, Who has so wondrously reached out for you. Don't get me wrong, by no means do I count myself an expert in all of this, but I've got my eye on the goal, where God is beckoning us onward—to Jesus. I'm off and running, and by the Grace of God, I'm not turning back (Philippians 3:12-14 MSG)!

When I slept in my Ford Focus the night I was unjustly removed from my home, I could have turned back then. The reason I could not was because I had allowed God's Grace to be sufficient for me and He was there with me, so I did not fear (Deuteronomy 31:6; Psalm 139:7). Besides, I was in great company, I didn't have to *imagine* how Joseph must have felt when he was betrayed by his brothers, thrown into a pit and later sold into slavery. He didn't know it at the time, but all he would suffer following their betrayal set him on a collision course with his destiny, which culminated in his becoming second in command over one of the greatest nations ever to exist on this earth.

His destiny strategically placed him in a position to save the lives of many people, including those who betrayed him. God is Awesome like that! When the enemy thinks he has you down for the count, God comes through with a one-two punch of Victory. Accordingly, instead of complaining about having to sleep in my little Ford, I praised Him and thanked Him for having the car and for His Divine Protection. Now I praise and thank Him for being able to ride high in my paid off Jeep Cherokee Latitude, a bigger, better, newer and more functional vehicle!

Now understand, I do not serve God because of what He can do for me! Knowing He can do anything, far more than I could ever think or imagine, guess or request in my wildest dreams is a huge draw! However, His exceeding and abundant blessings are only a collateral boon! I serve Him because I *Love* Him! He is not always conspicuous, nor does He bully us but He does graciously work, deeply and gently within those who Love Him and yield to His Spirit. In Loving Him, we overcome the world because of our Faith in Him, through His Son, Christ Jesus (Ephesians 3:20; 1 John 5:3-4 AMP)!

Do you now see what we have got? An unshakable Kingdom! Do you see how thankful we must be? Not only thankful, but brimming with Love, worship and deep reverence before God. For God is not an indifferent bystander. He is actively cleaning house, torching all that needs to burn. He will not quit until it's all cleansed. God Himself is Fire (Hebrews 12:28-29 MSG)! He will burn through all that's not of Him, so you can have a full and overflowing Life. A Life Full of Him and full of His Love.

FINAL THOUGHTS

Trust in and rely confidently on the Lord with all your heart and do not rely on your own insight or understanding. In all your ways know and acknowledge and recognize Him, and He will make your paths straight and smooth removing obstacles that block your way.
~ Proverbs 3:5-6 (AMP)

I do not know how God will work out your situation or circumstances. The uniqueness of who you are coupled with your willingness to be obedient to His Word will dictate the unswerving course in which He will direct your life. This is why you must Level up and be All in! God *will* help you, strengthen and empower you to Love. He will show you the way you must go. It may not be as clear as you may want it to be, but the more time you invest in Him, the more Faith's lens will sharpen and the path will become clearer. You must make up your mind to saturate your life with His Word because it is a map to the treasure of living a clean, productive and fulfilled life, rich in Love. Like the contemporary Christian Band Carrollton proclaims in their song, "Love builds bridges that cannot be burned, it speaks Truth that cannot be learned, its treasure we can never earn."

As you carefully read and study God's Word, a single-minded pursuit of Him will develop to aide you in not readily missing the road signs He's posted for you to find that Abundant Life. As you bank God's Promises in the vault of your heart, the less disposed you'll be to sin against Him and in turn undermine the ability to receive all of His Promises for you. God Speaks through His Word so don't believe everything you hear. Carefully weigh and examine what people tell you, including what you've read in this book. Go back, study out the scriptures posted because not everyone who talks about God comes from God, whatever comes to you to do must line up with His Word. This is how you know He is Speaking and not yourself or others (Psalm 119:11; 1 John 4:1 MSG).

Picture yourself as God's House. He used people, the inspired writers of His Word, as good architects to design and map out the blueprint, but He has made you the contractor! As Contractor, you are tasked to put up strong walls, oversee correct installations and implement exceptional design. Accordingly, take care as you build onto the foundation of His House! Remember, there is only one Foundation, the one already laid: Jesus Christ. Take particular care in picking out your building materials to frame out every part of His House because eventually, there is going to be an inspection. If you use cheap or inferior materials, like ideals that feel good to your flesh, but deny the divine, you will be found out (Hebrews 3:4-6 MSG).

The inspection will be thorough and rigorous because God has made plain His requirement and building codes. You won't get by with anything. If your work passes inspection, fine. If it does not, *your* part of the building—the part not in accord with God's Standards—will be torn out and started over. So, don't waste your time, energy and effort in building on what you've been given with inferior materials. Instead, complement your basic Faith with good character, spiritual understanding, alert discipline, passionate patience, reverent wonder, warm friendliness, and generous Love (2 Thessalonians 1:8 NLT; John 14:16 AMP; 2 Peter 1:5-9 MSG).

This book, while I pray was a great read for you, is intended to offer foundational designs in building your house with a sure, negotiable blueprint for finding and reveling in a Life hid with Christ in God concerning your individual choices, which profoundly impact your everyday life, as well as the lives of your family, friends and associates. Each dimension of the characteristics formed by applying God's Biblical Blueprints to your life, fit into and develop the others and are cultivated and solidified by Love. With these qualities active and growing in your life, you will always be on the move toward greatness. No day will pass without its reward as you mature in your knowledge and understanding of

our Savior, Jesus Christ, if you *choose* Him as Lord *of* your life
daily (Deuteronomy 30:20 NLT)!

Without these resources, you are blinded to what's right before
you, oblivious that your old sinful life has been wiped off the books.
You no longer have to hide. You must instead confirm God's invitation to you by giving your all to Him every moment of every day of
your life. Do not put it off another minute thinking you have time!
Do it now, day by day, step by step! Do this, and you'll have your
"house", your life on firm footing! The driveway paved and the way
wide open into the Eternal Kingdom of our Lord and Savior, Jesus
Christ. The needs and privileges that are yours in *this* life by way
of God's Kingdom, will be met in full. Do not allow preoccupation
with getting what you *want* out of life supersede your responding
to God's empowering you with what is best *for* your life.

People who don't know God and the Way He works fuss over
these things! You have been made free from such pettiness. Seek
to know both God and how He works by steeping your life in God-
reality, which inspires God-initiative, which brings about God-
provisions. Don't worry about missing out. Love will lead you
right where you need to be. Skillful and Godly Wisdom will enter
your heart and knowledge will be pleasant to your soul. Discretion
will watch over you, understanding and discernment will guard
you. You'll find all your everyday human concerns will be met as
well as an empowered life full of direction, strength and victory (1
Corinthians 3:9-15; 2 Peter 1:5-11; Proverbs 2:10,11; Matthew 6:33
MSG)! As the Band Carrollton further states, "(God's) Love is the
strongest way, (It's) tearing down walls and It breaks our chains!"

The opposite of Love is not hate—it is indifference. Apathy
or detached disinterest is the antipathy of Love as well as hate.
They are both strong entities existing on equal plains, which is
why there is a thin line between the two. In order to hate you must
hold the offense in your heart. You really only have to be offended
once. The challenge comes in remembering! To hate, you have to
remember over and over again. You must dwell on the infraction,
hold it securely in your heart and feed it constantly. It must be nurtured in order to thrive. This course of action has proven to impact

like a poison, causing hurts which blind and slowly eat away at your very soul.

Love is the same way only in the opposite. In order to Love, you must hold the contentment in your heart. You really only have to cherish once. The challenge comes in remembering! To Love, you have to remember over and over again. You must dwell on the treasured matter, hold it securely in your heart and feed it constantly. It must be nurtured in order to thrive. This course of action has proven to affect like a balm, healing hurts, clearing vision and restoring the soul.

You have the Power to choose which to remember, which to hold in your heart. On this walk of Faith, you're going to feel like quitting. In pressing toward the Mark for the Prize of the High Calling of God, you are going to struggle. While humbling yourself under His Mighty Hand so He may exalt you, you'll have days where you wonder, "Is this really worth it?" You'll have days when your adversary will use people (especially those close to you) to attempt to break you down, challenge your intelligence, and shake your claims of Faith in an attempt to abolish the Hope that lies within you. You'll have moments when you question your own salvation, and perhaps your very sanity (2 Corinthians 5:7; Philippians 3:14).

Nevertheless, every time you make the choice to choose Love over feelings, you'll rise! Not because you've defended yourself, but because you held fast to the Truth found only in the Gospel of Jesus Christ! You'll be ready to give a defense to anyone who asks you to account for the Hope and confident assurance that is within you, with gentleness and respect. As you rest in Him, God will be what *only He* can be in your life—your Strength and your Redeemer (Galatians 6:9; 1 Peter 3:15; Psalm19:14)!!

You'll rise at every opportunity you choose to honor God, with your trust and your confidence in His Integrity to back His Word. You'll rise, even when the enemy comes in like a flood because you choose God—He *will* lift up His Standard against him! You'll rise, because the fact that you're struggling for Christ's sake, you may also share in His Glory as you strive for His Excellence! You'll rise, because your Strength is no longer your own but Christ Jesus' working through you, making even the smallest difference in the lives of all whose lives you touch with Truth (Isaiah 59:19; 2 Timothy 2:12; Ephesians 3:16; 2 Corinthians 3:2 AMP).

You must also have a strong prayer life and I'm not talking about a "Thank you Jesus, Amen!" I'm talking about no holds barred, down and dirty, real deal conversations with the Most High God (1 Thessalonians 5:16-18, Romans 12:12, Colossians 4:2, Ephesians 6:18, Luke 21:36)! You know the kind! If you are female, the kind of girlfriend conversations beginning with Ben and Jerry's and ending with tears, scattered tissues and you both closer than you were before you started. If you are male, the kind of Bromance where you bond on the court playing basketball, some other sport or over a sweaty workout at the gym, the point is— God's time is more important.

He should be your "Go to" Person, your All in All! Your life will advance and gain upward motion when you get your priorities straight as a Believer. You will *say* the right things when the Truth is in your head, but you will *do* the right things when Truth is in your heart! Whether you are All-In for two minutes or for twenty-eight years, God plays no favorites! It makes no difference who you are or where you're from. If you want an Abundant Life and are ready to do what is necessary to get it, the door is open to do just that. The Power is not in how long you've been All-In, but in how you *stay* All-In (Acts 10:34; Romans 2:11; Luke 20:21 AMP)!!!

It is momentous to receive Christ as Savior of your life, but is it metamorphic to *make* Him Lord *of* your life! God is no respecter of persons! He will move for you according to your Faith so properly frame your Faith through the study of and obedience to His Word and Love will reveal the way. Make Him your Necessary Food and not the whims, doctrines and dictates of a bankrupt, corrupt culture designed to waylay and misdirect you (Acts 10:34; Matthew 9:29; Job 23:12; Romans 12:2).

Allow God to fill you, Direct and Guide you by choosing Love's Way over worldly ideas, ingrained habits or generational hang-ups. Doing so is the difference between a life lived on auto pilot and a life lived on purpose. When you live life on purpose, it will cease being a burden you bear and become an adventure you seek! Level

Up, plug in, let go and let God because Tina was mistaken, Love is *not* a secondhand emotion!

God is Love and Jesus is the Cornerstone of Love upon which we are to build our lives (1 John 4:8; Ephesians 2:20). Choosing to Love is choosing Life. Choosing Life is choosing God—which means Love is all you need! Carrollton's song triumphantly ends with a galvanized Truth stating, "Even in this darkness Hope will rise again, when we lay down our weapons we will [***Let Love Win**]*!" The carnal weapons driven by jealously, hate, greed and envy will become inert under the great, equalizing Power of Love. To answer more accurately, what Tina Turner so eloquently asked decades ago, "What's Love got to do with it?" *THIS* is what Love has got to do with it, with life—GOD, and He is *EVERYTHING*!

CPSIA information can be obtained
at www.ICGtesting.com
Printed in the USA
LVHW030548180820
663484LV00005B/295